K9 PERSONAL PROTECTION

Other titles in the *K9 Professional Training series*

K9 Behavior Basics, 2nd ed.
K9 Search and Rescue, 2nd ed.
K9 Schutzhund Training, 2nd ed.
K9 Scent Training (forthcoming 2015)
K9 Decoys and Aggression (forthcoming 2015)
K9 Explosive Training (forthcoming 2016)

Other K9 titles from Brush Education

Aggression Control
K9 Complete Care
K9 Explosive Detection
K9 Fraud!
K9 Officer's Manual
K9 Professional Tracking
K9 Scent Detection
K9 Suspect Discrimination
K9 Working Breeds
Police Officer's Guide to K9 Searches

K9 PERSONAL PROTECTION

A Manual for Training Reliable Protection Dogs

Second edition

Dr. Resi Gerritsen
Ruud Haak

K9 Professional Training series

An imprint of
Brush Education Inc.

Brush Education Inc.
www.brusheducation.ca
contact@brusheducation.ca

Editorial: Meaghan Craven
Cover design: John Luckhurst, Cover image: Shutterstock, Victoria Antonova
Interior design: Carol Dragich, Dragich design

Printed and manufactured in Canada

Library and Archives Canada Cataloguing in Publication
Gerritsen, Resi, author
K9 personal protection : a manual for training reliable protection dogs / Dr. Resi Gerritsen, Ruud Haak. — Second edition.

(K9 professional training series)

Revision of: K9 personal protection : a manual for training reliable protection dogs / Resi Gerritsen and Ruud Haak. — Calgary : Detselig Enterprises, ©2002. Includes bibliographical references. Issued in print and electronic formats.
ISBN 978-1-55059-588-8 (pbk.).—ISBN 978-1-55059-589-5 (pdf).—ISBN 978-1-55059-590-1 (mobi).—ISBN 978-1-55059-591-8 (epub)

1. Watchdogs—Training.   I. Haak, Ruud, author   II. Title.   III. Series: K9 professional training series

SF428.8.G465 2014   636.7′0886   C2014-906864-6
                                            C2014-906865-4

Contents

Introduction vii

Raising and Training

1   Conditions for Success 3

2   Breeds for Protection Work 17

3   Training Methods... 49

4   Our Relationship with Dogs............................ 58

5   Basic Education and Exercises......................... 67

6   Stopping Bad Behavior 77

Obedience

7   Training for Heelwork 91

8   Training the Sit..100

9   Training the Down...107

10 Training the Stay...113

11 Training the Stand and Touching 120

12 Training the Recall..127

13 Training the Send Away 134

14 Practical Obedience 140

Protection

15 The Dutch Police Dog Test..149

16 Decoy and Dog...169

17 Raising for Protection 188

18 Basic Exercises for Protection 200

19 Training for Protection 205

    Epilogue: Pets and the Working Dog 227

    Appendix: Dutch, German, and English Commands.................231

    Bibliography...237

    About the Authors 239

Introduction

It's impossible to imagine life today without professionally trained guard, sentry, and police dogs. Dog sports like Schutzhund and Ringsport also champion reliable protection work, and there are many privately owned companion dogs that work as protection dogs.

The successful training of a reliable protection dog doesn't start, as is often thought, with bite work, but rather with a good education and obedience exercises. People who don't agree and who don't have a good relationship with their dog and have not valued obedience training, sometimes start training very young dogs to do bite work and thus spoil their dogs forever. The dangers that accompany bite work are so great that we emphatically advise against starting this type of training with dogs younger than 12 months. If a dog starts bite work at too young an age, he will invariably be a frightened dog or a totally aggressive dog that is impossible to control. Therefore, bite training should begin only when the dog is physically and mentally ready for it. As mentioned, the proper age for bite work is almost never younger than 12 months and often as old as 18 months.

While you wait to implement bite work into your training schedule, thoroughly teach your dog obedience exercises until he is a year old. During this period, you can also start training him to perform the preparatory protection exercises, as mentioned in Chapter 17, "Raising for Protection."

Every dog that is safe in and suitable to our communities—definitely including reliable protection dogs—must have mastered certain basic skills. For instance, dogs must:

- not pull the leash;
- on command: sit, lie down, stand, stay, and come; and
- display normal behavior with humans and other animals.

To help you ensure your protection dog has these basic skills, we clearly describe how to train for them in the Obedience section of this book, before we write comprehensively about protection training. As in the real world, obedience comes before protection.

We have also presented the PH-1 test of the Royal Dutch Police Dog Association (KNPV) because it is intended to assess dogs trained not only for the police service and police tasks but also for their potential to be reliable protection dogs. In Chapter 16, "Decoy and Dog," we discuss, among other things, the behavior of the decoy and that of the dog, as well as the important warm-up and cool-down exercises that don't take much time but prevent injuries.

However, before you get into the details associated with training, start at the beginning of this book with Chapter 1, "Conditions for Success," and Chapter 2, "Breeds for Protection Work," in which you will find a discussion about the most likely breeds to train for protection work based on our comprehensive training experiences with those breeds.

—Dr. Resi Gerritsen and Ruud Haak

Disclaimer

Raising and Training

1

Conditions for Success

There are sometimes misunderstandings about the suitability of dogs for protection training. Often people accept without question that every dog that is a so-called working dog or herding dog is able to complete the special training for protection work. This belief is, however, not true, and therefore we have to make careful choices when selecting dogs for this role. Nervous and frightened dogs, for instance, should not be considered. With a lot of perseverance, an experienced handler may achieve something with such a dog, but for the dog herself the training and work will mostly be a mental torment, and this will be expressed sooner or later in serious disorders.

Only mentally and physically healthy dogs can successfully undergo this heavy training. For example, some dog breeds tend to have several problems, such as hip and elbow dysplasia, which prevent the normal movements of the dog. As well, other hereditary, physical defects such as epilepsy and eye disorders also make affected dogs absolutely unsuitable for protection work.

Physical Qualities

A successful protection dog should:

- be absolutely healthy, and sound in life and limb;
- walk and move correctly and quickly;

Only mentally and physically healthy dogs can successfully undergo protection training.

- have a strong and muscled body;
- have an optimal sense of smell, sight, and hearing;
- have very good and powerful teeth;
- be in optimal condition and have stamina;
- have strong legs and feet with strong soles;
- be adapted to the weather and climate in which she has to work;
- have a coat suitable for her climate; and
- preferably have a shoulder height between 21 and 28 inches (55 and 70 cm).

Missing the mark . . .

Mental Characteristics

The most important mental characteristic that a protection dog should have is intelligence. We distinguish between three forms of intelligence: the instinctive, the practical, and the adaptive. By *instinctive intelligence*, we mean all hereditary skills and behavior, such as the hunting drive: every pup runs after a moving object. By *practical intelligence*, we mean the speed with which, and the degree to which, the dog conforms to the desires of the handler: roughly said, how quickly and how correctly the dog learns the different exercises. *Adaptive intelligence* can be divided into two abilities: learning proficiency, or how quickly the dog develops adequate behavior in a new situation; and problem-solving ability, or the dog's ability to choose the correct behavior to solve a problem she encounters.

Strength of Character

Protection dogs must also have strong character. They must behave in a self-confident manner and be free of nervousness, fear, or jumpiness. Sudden and unexpected "prickles," like gunfire, traffic noise, or waving flags, will not bring these dogs out of balance.

Temperament

A dog's temperament is expressed in her psychological skills and her reactions to different prickles from the environment. The more lively a dog is and the more intensive her response to her surroundings, the more full of temperament she is. The slower and the less she reacts to her environment, the less temperament the dog has. In the strong presence of certain drives (for instance, the guard drive), we can see dogs full of temperament focusing intently when an appropriate, small prickle in the environment occurs (for instance, a person approaching from far away). For the protection dog, such a temperament is important because it contributes to her being happy, attentive, and always active.

It is important to recognize the difference between a dog full of temperament and a nervous dog. Some people want dogs that are immediately itching to react when something happens. They say such dogs have temperament, but this is not true; rather, these dogs are three-quarters nervous, as well as sharp (see page 9). If a dog is not full of temperament, she is not able to complete the training to become a protection dog.

To do protection work, dogs must be in good health and have a great deal of stamina.

Composure

A protection dog must stay absolutely calm and show self-confidence, even when placed in strange circumstances. She must quietly observe any situation without fear or anxiety. Regardless of the situation—among people, in a town, amongst traffic, or at an event—the dog has to stay calm. Only then is she able to act at the right moment in the right way.

Reliability

The protection dog's behavior must be consistent and reliable, so her performance is without surprises. Suddenly lunging at playing children or at adults, or displaying aggression toward housemates or even to you, the handler, causes serious damage to the acceptability of dogs in our society.

Dogs that are too independent and "resist" are also disturbing, and they are not in favor for training as protection dogs. As well, dogs that are "everybody's friend" are not always ideal either.

Instead, the dog that is a bit reserved and shows an appropriate, natural sharpness can be a good dog for our goal if she is absolutely reliable. She must know how to assess the situation and act only when she receives the commands of her handler.

A protection dog guards a jeweler's shop.

Toughness

By *toughness* we mean the ability to suffer unpleasant prickles or events—such as pain, punishment, or defeat in a fight—without being put off for even a moment, and the ability to forget these issues just as quickly (showing low sensitivity). A dog that can calmly undergo such torments will be able to carry out your commands, even if she is hurt or in pain. Such a dog will not be deterred by an attack, for instance, by a decoy (the person who helps train dogs for protection work), nor be upset by a decoy's yelling, shooting, or touches with the soft or rattan stick.

A soft dog is the tough dog's opposite. The soft dog is strongly affected by unpleasant prickles, events, or frightening circumstances, and will avoid such situations or prickles in the future (showing high sensitivity). Softness must not, however, be confused with fear of pain. Some dogs are very sensitive to pain and will squeal at the littlest pinch, such as an injection. But they will not lose their confidence against the one who causes the pain. Fear of pain will not necessarily influence these dogs' willingness to work, because during the work the

It is vital that the decoy correctly judge the direction and manner in which the dog is approaching him. Decoys must work safely with potential protection dogs so that they and the dogs are not injured.

dogs normally are so caught up in their duties that they don't recognize the pain.

Courage and Sharpness

Courageous dogs step into dangerous situations without any pressure from outside, and they stay there, even when the situation would otherwise encourage them to flee as a result of their instinct for self-preservation.

Sharpness is the inclination of dogs to react in a hostile way to unexpected prickles; with sharpness, self-preservation plays a big role. Dogs in which sharpness is developed too strongly, and that also show a lack of courage, tend to bite out of fear.

With regard to courage and sharpness, there are four types of dogs:

a) Courageous–Sharp
b) Courageous–Not Sharp
c) Not Courageous–Sharp
d) Not Courageous–Not Sharp

Courage and sharpness complement each other sometimes, but they can also be opposites.

The basic characteristic of sharpness is the hostile attitude of the dog toward the unknown, and it can be based as much on self-assurance and an inherent fighting spirit as on uncertainty, distrust, and fear. In the first case, sharpness is inherited; in the second case, it is a quality acquired through training and a need for self-defense. With sharpness, the dog's drive for self-preservation figures prominently. The stronger this drive for self-preservation is developed in the animal, the greater her sharpness will be.

Because courage is understood to be the quality a dog has that allows her to stay in dangerous situations without pressure from outside, the drive for self-preservation does not come into play with courageous dogs.

We can describe the four types as follows:

A) COURAGEOUS–SHARP

The dog moves in a hostile manner in the direction of what she sees as a danger. She displays a high tail; barking or a combative, open mouth; and bristled back hairs. The dog expresses no fear and is ready for a fight.

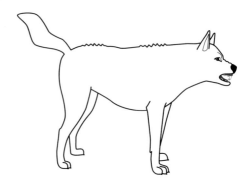

B) COURAGEOUS–NOT SHARP

The dog isn't combative but is indifferent or curious, showing no sign of fear. She either approaches the unusual with interested tail wagging or ignores the stimulus entirely. The dog is fearless without hostility.

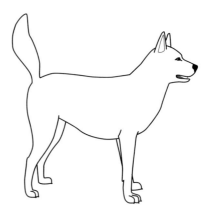

C) NOT COURAGEOUS–SHARP

The dog expresses anxious willingness to defend herself, displaying bristled back hairs, usually with a hanging but sometimes with a high tail, and growling, showing the teeth, or barking. The dog withdraws from the area of danger and expresses anxiety and hostility.

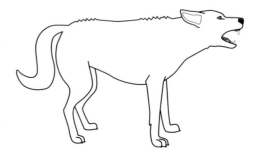

D) NOT COURAGEOUS–NOT SHARP

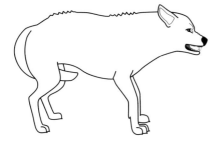

The dog is anxious and ready to flee but lacks a hostile attitude. The dog withdraws with her tail pulled between her legs, sometimes with a crouched body or a crooked back, and in extreme cases screaming in fear or urinating. This dog is anxious without hostility.

SUITABILITY

It can happen that both characteristics, courage and sharpness, are mistakenly thought to be present in a dog, but instead breeding has combined the wrong characteristics and the results in training disappoint. It can also happen that a handler (whether aware of it or not) will try to make "not courageous–sharp" dogs sharper. An artificial increase of sharpness is always unsuccessful, however, because the dog will never be able to distinguish between apparent and real danger.

In our experience, training a protection dog whose type is described under either c) or d) will always result in disappointment. In the interests of the dog and you, the handler, it is always best to exclude such dogs from protection dog training.

A reliable protection dog must have a great basic confidence in humans and in herself. The ideal dog for this work is one that is balanced, reliable, self-confident, tough, and courageous, and that has an adapted, natural sharpness. Dogs that are not well balanced, not self-confident, not courageous, or too sharp will normally fail in this training.

Other Characteristics

Other characteristics we demand of ideal protection dogs include devotion to the handler and family and a willingness to work, because a dog you have to wake up for work is not the right one for this job. A dog that likes to work makes a lot of noise and shows interest when she sees that you're getting ready to go. What is also, maybe even more, important is that the dog has to show both before and during work an almost tireless willingness to work. To be able to do this, she must be in good health and have a great deal of stamina. In short, a dog in which you can see a definite willingness to work and that needs no encouragement to continue and concentrate on her work is a good one for protection work.

Other important characteristics include attentiveness and protection drive, or the inclination of the dog to protect her pack mates, in this case, humans, against attacks.

Male or Female?

Both genders have their particular advantages and disadvantages. Males as well as females can be friendly, devoted, and attractive. It has been observed that males perform more energetically than females, but they are also sometimes more obstinate. Normally, a male is bigger and more powerful, often more extroverted and strongly interested in other dogs, especially females in heat.

Females are often a bit more focused on their handlers, and they can also defend their handlers and families with a great fierceness. They are sometimes a bit snappish, but they are often more homey than males, although not always when they are in heat. The female's reproductive cycle starts when she is between nine and 12 months and brings her into heat twice per year, during which time blood secretions from her swollen vulva can stain your carpet. (Males can also be "messy," secreting fluid from the penis if they have a common disorder called balanoposthitis, an inflammation of the penis and prepuce.) When in heat, a female dog becomes a bit more restless than normal, and she loses drops of blood regularly for 10 to 14 days. When the bleeding stops, normally around the 12th day after the beginning of the heat, she is receptive to males. A female will be in heat for about three weeks, and during that time contact with males should be avoided, except, of course, if she is to be bred. There are remedies out there that suppress the natural odor of a female in heat or mask some of her scent. However, many (police) service dogs are spayed to avoid all upsets caused by the reproductive cycle. Before, during, and after being in heat, females are often less able to carry out their protection duties because their physical condition is weaker than usual. As well, before, during, and after being in heat, females are more sensitive to influences in their environment.

A Good Match for You

Not all dog breeds will match your personality, and not every individual dog fits every person or household. Some affectionate dog breeds, for instance those with a strong "will to please" such as the German or Belgian shepherds, normally have a gentle character and submit themselves easily to humans. Such a sensitive dog can easily be upset by a bad education. That said, some shepherds do not display this kind of character and are instead tough and obstinate.

Some dogs have a bubbly personality and want to see and hear everything that happens in their surroundings. They breathe down their handlers' necks all day long. If such a dog is sent to her place, she will look aggrieved but still be absolutely attentive to the movements of her handler. It is not possible for everyone to work with a sensitive or tough and obstinate dog. And someone who cannot stand to have his dog hang around the whole day, of course, has to carefully choose when selecting a dog. It is important to remember that dogs also have certain requirements from their handlers.

Someone who is a bit short-tempered and dominant had better leave a dog with a sensitive character alone; this person would destroy such a dog in a short time. A quiet person who has the necessary patience will better serve a sensitive dog and with patience will have a protection dog that learns quickly and will be reasonably watchful. We must never confuse sensitivity in dogs with nervousness or shyness. Sensitive dogs are easily ruined when handled in the wrong way.

Bull terriers can work well as protection dogs.

There are also dogs that are "young at heart" for a long time and therefore need a long time to mature. Handling such a dog in a tough way too early will result in a damaged dog; "young" dogs just cannot handle the pressure that accompanies protection training.

In the end, it is best to choose a breed that matches your own character and lifestyle and never make a choice based only on the external appearance of a certain breed.

Character Traits

A pedigreed dog doesn't just happen; she is the result of a careful selection of certain (working) traits, and those traits must match you if you are to work with her. The breeds known as working dogs or herding dogs were originally bred for many different purposes. The characters and typical behaviors of these breeds are often very different.

We know protection dogs that were originally cattle dogs, guarding herds of cattle and escorting them independently to various locations. Such dogs include Rottweilers and the Bouvier des Flandres, for instance. Other breeds that work well as protection dogs are ones from the group of shepherd dogs, which originally tended flocks of sheep; on the instructions of the shepherd, these dogs kept the sheep together and moved them in the determined direction. In this group we include, among others, the German, Belgian, and Dutch shepherd dogs.

Most cattle dogs are a bit tougher than shepherd dogs, and they have, in our experience, less inclination to spontaneous co-operation with the handler. This is because cattle dogs were bred to work independently, with big animals. These dogs, therefore, still exhibit an independent character. Training a cattle dog will, in the beginning, be a bit more difficult than training a shepherd dog. A cattle dog is often not as easy to motivate for certain exercises, and if you try to over-repeat the same exercise with a cattle dog, you usually end up with a dog that refuses to work anymore. However, even though it often takes longer to teach cattle dogs to perform certain exercises quickly and happily in comparison to shepherd dogs, we have seen many Bouviers and Rottweilers that are excellent workers.

We have found that once a cattle dog reaches a high level in protection training, she remembers what she has been taught better than a shepherd dog, and she often works out the instructions more promptly, even if she hasn't trained for a while. A good example of this was a Bouvier that didn't work in obedience for about two years, and in spite of that worked out the former learned exercises very well. This is the opposite of certain shepherd dogs, which, if they haven't trained for a long time, show that they have pushed the learned exercises to the background, and are not or are barely able to work out the instructions. However, shepherd dogs are also often more willing to work and more diligent than their cattle dog counterparts, and for physical reasons they can stay in active service longer. Whereas a lot of cattle dogs finish their tasks at about eight years, we have seen that, for example, Malinois can work until they are 12 years old or sometimes even older.

In the next chapter, we will discuss some breeds that are suitable for training as protection dogs and also give you a view of the special abilities of these breeds. Of course, our survey is not complete, and other breeds can also do well in protection work, such as the Akita, American Staffordshire terrier, Kuvasz, Rhodesian ridgeback, and Briard, among others, just as, of course, different non-pedigreed and mixed-breed dogs can be suitable for the work.

Independent of the choice of breed, when choosing a future protection dog out of a litter, always make sure that the dog descends from working-dog lines, which means that the parents, and if possible also the grandparents and other ancestors, were trained and have a proven ability to work with people. Most dogs descending from show lines, in spite of their good looks, cannot deliver the achievements required for protection dog training.

2

Breeds for Protection Work

The German Shepherd Dog

This breed may, without exaggeration, be called the best-known dog breed in the world, and yet, the German shepherd dog (in German: *Deutscher Schäferhund*) as a distinct breed is just over a century old. At the end of the 19th century, all sorts of shepherd and farm dogs in Europe were, in outlook and behavior, rather different from each other, depending on the regions in which they were working. There was no standard type that could claim the name German shepherd dog, and it was to the credit of the founders of this breed, Rittmeister Max von Stephanitz and Arthur Meyer, that this middle-sized shepherd dog came into being. From the beginning, this breed was used as a service dog by the police, customs, and military. The breed is particularly admired because of its achievements during both World Wars. Below we list the characteristics cited by the official breed standard, as well as characteristics we have noticed while training this breed.

GENERAL APPEARANCE

The first impression of a good German shepherd dog is that of a strong, agile, well-muscled animal, alert and full of life. The dog's body is slightly long in comparison to her height, and she

The German shepherd dog is the best-known breed in the world.

is powerful; square or leggy dogs are not standard. The erect ears are moderately pointed; cropped or hanging ears are a big fault. The color can be black, iron-gray, or ash-gray, either as the solid color or with regular brown, tan, or light-gray markings, also with a black saddle or dark sable ("wolf-color"). The ideal dog has a double coat of medium length. The outer coat is thick and made of straight, coarse, close-lying hairs; too short and too long hair is undesirable.

SIZE
The desired height for males at the top of the highest point of the shoulder blade is 24 to 26 inches (60–65 cm) and for females 22 to 24 inches (55–60 cm).

CHARACTER
The breed has a distinct personality marked by a direct and fearless, but not hostile, expression, self-confidence and a certain aloofness that does not allow for immediate and indiscriminate friendships. The dog must be approachable, and she must quietly stand her ground and show confidence and willingness to meet overtures without herself making them. She is poised, but when the occasion demands, eager and alert; she is both fit and willing to serve in her capacity as companion, watchdog, guide dog, herding dog, or guardian, whatever the circumstances may demand. The

dog must not be timid, shrinking behind her master or handler; she should not be nervous, looking about or upward with an anxious expression or showing nervous reactions, such as tucking of the tail, to strange sounds or sights. Lack of confidence under any circumstances is not typical of good character. The ideal German shepherd dog is a working animal with an incorruptible character combined with a body and gait suitable for the arduous work that constitutes her primary purpose.

OUR TRAINING EXPERIENCES

The German shepherd dog needs close contact with her handler and his or her family; she also requires a lot of exercise and tasks to perform. Because too much attention was paid to the exterior of this breed in recent years, a lot of the original practical value has been lost. That said, the German shepherd dog is a devoted and handler-oriented dog with a lot of "will to please." Generally, these dogs are outstanding examples of the working dog; however, we must say (and it is a pity) that this breed does show a lot of defects, mentally as well as physically.

In training, many German shepherd dogs display apathy. However, if one has a fine, correctly bred dog, then one can without any doubt achieve excellent results with her in protection work. Because German shepherd dogs are focused on their handlers, the good ones are highly motivated in training. She will be much less tempted by distractions in her surroundings, and because of that, she is able to diligently concentrate on her tasks. In a proper training environment, she can work out her exercises quickly, correctly, and with a good temperament, and she also shows excellent work in the defense exercises. However, the mental ability of a lot of modern-day German shepherd dogs we have worked with is not reliable, so that is a problem you might encounter.

Belgian Shepherd Dogs

At the end of the 19th century in Belgium, a middle-sized, nimble, alert, and guarding shepherd dog was developed. This dog had a great deal of stamina and was both strongly focused on her handler and capable of working independently if the situation demanded it. Around 1890, the Belgian professor Adolphe Reul of the Belgian Veterinary School in Brussels listed the native (shepherd) dogs and promoted their purebred raising. It took a lot of time before there was agreement on the colors and hair varieties of these typical shepherd dogs.

In Belgian shepherd dogs (in Flemish: *Belgische Herdershonden*), we distinguish between four closely related shepherd dogs that have three types of coat: the Belgian sheepdog or Groenendael, the Belgian Tervuren, the Belgian Laekenois, and the best-known type of the breed, the Belgian Malinois. The latter has been used from the beginning of the 20th century very intensively for guarding and police tasks. The Malinois is still one of the best working dogs, found more and more everywhere in the world in service to police, customs, and army. Below we list the characteristics cited by the official breed standard, as well as characteristics we have noticed while training this breed.

GENERAL APPEARANCE
The first impression of the Belgian shepherd dog is that of a balanced, square dog, elegant in appearance, with an exceedingly proud carriage of the head and neck. She is strong, agile, well-muscled, alert, and full of life. Her head is finely chiseled, and the highly set, triangular ears are stiff and erect.

SIZE
Males should be 24 to 26 inches (60–66 cm) in height and females 22 to 24 inches (56–62 cm), measured at the withers.

VARIETIES
The Groenendael has, just like the Tervuren (below), a long, straight, and abundant coat with a collarette around the neck. The Groenendael is completely black.

The Tervuren, like the Groenendael, is a long-haired dog. The rich fawn to russet mahogany with black overlay color, which is required for the Malinois (below), is also favored in the Tervuren. The coat is characteristically double pigmented: the tip of each fawn hair is black. A black mask and a minimum of eight pigmented points is standard: black at both ears, both upper eyelids, both upper lips, and both under lips.

The Laekenois has a rough, wire-haired coat. Unlike the long-haired Belgian shepherd dogs, the coat on the head of the Laekenois is also longer. This harsh, wiry, dry, and straight coat is reddish fawn with black shading, principally on the muzzle and tail.

The Malinois has a comparatively short, straight coat—hard enough to be weather resistant—with a dense undercoat. The hair should be very short on her head, ears, and lower legs. The hair is somewhat longer around the neck, where it forms a collarette, and on the tail and backs of the thighs. The basic coloring is rich fawn to mahogany, with black tips on the hairs giving an overlay appearance. Other colors are not standard. The Malinois has a black mask and the same pigmentation points as the Tervuren. The tips of the toes may be white, and a small white spot on the breastbone/prosternum is permitted but should not to extend to the neck. Other white markings are faulty according to the breed standard.

The Malinois is the short-coated Belgian shepherd dog.

Belgian Sheepdog

CHARACTER

The Belgian sheepdog, or Groenendael, should reflect the qualities of intelligence, courage, alertness, and devotion to her handler. To her inherent aptitude as a guardian of flocks should be added protectiveness of the person and property of her handler. She should be watchful, attentive, and always in motion when not under command. In her relationship with humans, she should be observant and vigilant with strangers but not apprehensive. She should not show fear or shyness, nor should she show viciousness by unwarranted or unprovoked attack. With those she knows well, she is most affectionate and friendly, zealous of their attention, and very possessive.

OUR TRAINING EXPERIENCES

The Groenendaels we have met in training are indeed willing to work and easy to motivate, but they are very active, tending toward nervousness. In our opinion, they often lack courage, sharpness, and hardness. The dogs don't quickly forget a bad experience and are affected by it for a long time. We have found that many of these dogs cannot endure the threats that accompany training with a decoy. Maybe the reason for this is that Groenendaels are trained less frequently, and in the breeding too much attention is given to beauty.

Belgian Tervuren

CHARACTER

In her relationship with humans, the Belgian Tervuren is observant and vigilant with strangers but not apprehensive. She does not show fear or shyness, nor does she display viciousness by unwarranted or unprovoked attacks. She must be approachable and yet stand her ground and show confidence in meeting overtures without making them herself. With those she knows well, she is most affectionate and friendly, zealous for their attention, and very possessive.

OUR TRAINING EXPERIENCES

The Tervurens we see in training are willing to work and easy to motivate, but they are also very active, tending toward nervousness, and they often lack courage, sharpness, and hardness for the same reasons as the Groenendael. Again, we have found few of these dogs that can endure training with a decoy.

Belgian Laekenois

CHARACTER

The Belgian Laekenois is a watchful and active dog, bursting with energy, and always ready to leap into action. In addition to being innately skilled at guarding flocks, she also possesses all of the highly prized qualities of the best property guard dogs. She does not hesitate to stubbornly and keenly protect her owner. She brings together all of the qualities necessary for a shepherd: guard, defense, and service. Her lively, alert temperament and confident nature—she shows no fear or aggressiveness—should be obvious in her stance and the proud attentive expression in her sparkling eyes.

OUR TRAINING EXPERIENCES

About half a century ago, the Laekenois were seen very often in training. They were at that time very sharp, tough, and courageous dogs, which, unfortunately, became unpopular in training and fell out of favor. These days, they are rarely seen in training, and the famous character they displayed 50 years ago has been lost to breeding for "prettiness."

Belgian Malinois

CHARACTER

Correct temperament is essential to the working character of the Belgian Malinois. The breed is confident, exhibiting neither shyness nor aggressiveness in new situations. The dog may be reserved with strangers but is affectionate with her own people. She is naturally protective of her owner's person and property without being overly aggressive. The Malinois possesses a strong desire to work and is quick and responsive to commands from her owner.

OUR TRAINING EXPERIENCES

The Malinois is active and sometimes a bit busy, willing to work but because of her enthusiasm, she sometimes is a bit difficult to train correctly. She is particularly eager to learn, but at the same time a bit sloppy. Our Malinois dogs, like others we have known from training, are excellent protection dogs with powerful and convincing bites. They are particularly easy to motivate in bite training. The character of the Malinois is rather tough, which means that after a bad experience she will recover—with a kind word from her handler—and continue to work enthusiastically and with good temperament. The toughness of the Malinois, however, can also contribute to a bad education. When growing up, the Malinois is very sensitive to the attitude and mood of her handler and must be approached quietly and raised with the necessary understanding. Only that way can she develop properly and become an excellent adult working dog.

Dutch Shepherd Dogs

The Dutch shepherd dog (in Dutch: *Hollandse Herdershond*) comes from a line of dogs that herd sheep and guard small farms in the southern part of the Netherlands, especially in the province of Brabant near the Belgian border. Until 1839 Belgium was a part of Holland, and so the Dutch shepherd dog is strongly related to both Belgian and German shepherd dogs. The latter became, over the years, more "embellished," but the Dutch shepherd dog remains an honest, "ordinary" dog with a sober outlook. Because of the work this dog does, she has been able to take on a variety of tasks, including work with police, in Schutzhund and Ring-sport, and as a protection dog. She is a typical "one-man" dog and will keep in close contact with her handler. She is, however, also a dog that needs clear leadership, otherwise she will determine for herself what she is to do. Note that this dog needs an activity-filled environment. Below we list the characteristics cited by the official breed standard, as well as characteristics we have noticed while training this breed.

GENERAL APPEARANCE

The Dutch shepherd dog is of medium size and is strong and muscular. She is very active and has a keen expression and clear temperament. The head is a wedge, rather small, between the small, upright, triangular ears, which are set high on the skull. She is fairly square in conformation (with a height to length ratio of 9:10) and an easy mover, using her legs in a supple manner. The breed standard demands normal, moderate angulation of the fore- and hindquarters. There are three varieties, which differ in coat structure and color.

The double coat of the short-coated variety is reasonably hard, but not too short. The permitted colors are gold brindle (dark brindle on a tan background) or silver brindle (dark brindle on a gray background). Preferably, the short-coated variety has a black mask.

The wire-coated variety has a harsh, dense, wiry coat covering the whole body, with, except on the head, a woolly, dense under-coat. The head has a big mustache, beard, and rough eyebrows. Besides the colors gold brindle and silver brindle, in the wire-coated variety blue-gray and salt-and-pepper are also permitted.

Required in the rough-coated variety is a long, straight coat, with abundant feathering, trousers, and tail fringe. For color, the same is in force as for the short-coated variety: gold or silver brindle. The rough-coated variety had almost disappeared by around 1930 but has since come back.

SIZE

The desired height for males at the top of the highest point of the shoulder blade is 22.5 to 24.5 inches (57–62 cm) and for females 22 to 24 inches (55–60 cm).

The short-coated Dutch shepherd has an attractive gold or silver brindle coat.

CHARACTER
The Dutch shepherd dog is affectionate, obedient, docile, watchful, prepared, loyal, reliable, undemanding, ever alert, active, talented, and has great stamina and a real "shepherd" character.

OUR TRAINING EXPERIENCES
The Dutch shepherd dog is quieter of character than the Malinois, but just like the latter, it is a "think ahead" type that already knows what the next exercise will require and often wants to start with that. The stable character of this dog and her great devotion to her handler is remarkable. The work that, especially, the short-coated variety shows in police dog training is very good. The dog is incorruptible, a bit distrusting of strangers, but very loyal to her family and good-natured with children. Her natural watchfulness makes her a good guard of hearth and home. She works cheerfully but needs an appropriate upbringing. A Dutch shepherd puppy needs and deserves an honest, quiet, and strict education to become a stable dog. The rough-coated variety is more sensitive in character than the other two varieties and is therefore less suitable for protection dog training.

Rottweiler

This breed, named for the German city of Rottweil, was used primarily for guarding and driving cattle but also for guarding the farm and family. Besides cattle, the Rottweiler also had to watch her master's money bag, which was often bound around the dog's neck for safekeeping—especially if the master wanted to celebrate a good sale. At the end of the 19th century, when dog breeds were selected for the police service, the Rottweiler was tested for that purpose. The results of tests made it clear that this dog was very reliable for the requirements of the police service. In 1910 the Rottweiler was officially recognized in Germany as a police dog. Today, breeders still strive for a very powerful dog, which results in a sturdy figure that both suggests a kind of nobility and is useful for a working dog. Below we list the characteristics cited by the official breed standard, as well as characteristics we have noticed while training this breed.

GENERAL APPEARANCE

The ideal Rottweiler is a medium-large, robust, and powerful dog, black with clearly defined rust markings. The breed's compact and substantial build denotes great strength, agility, and endurance. Males are characteristically more massive throughout with a larger frame and heavier bone structure than females. The skull is broad and the ears are of medium size, triangular in shape and pendant; when carried alertly, the ears are level with the top of the skull and appear to broaden it. The outer coat is straight, coarse, dense, of medium length, and lies flat. The color is always black with rust-to-mahogany markings, located as follows: a spot over each eye; on the cheeks, as a strip around each side of the muzzle, but not on the bridge of the nose; on the throat; a triangular mark on both sides of the prosternum; on the forelegs from the carpus downward to the toes; on the inside of the rear legs, showing down the front of the stifle and broadening out to the front of the rear legs from the hocks to the toes; and under the tail.

The Rottweiler is a medium-large, robust, and powerful dog.

SIZE

The desired height for males at the top of the highest point of the shoulder blade is 24 to 27 inches (61–68 cm) and for females 22 to 25 inches (56–63 cm); the preferred size is mid-range for each sex.

CHARACTER

The Rottweiler is a calm, confident, and courageous dog with a self-assured aloofness that does not lend itself to immediate and indiscriminate friendships. A Rottweiler is self-confident and responds quietly and with a wait-and-see attitude to influences in her environment. She has an inherent desire to protect home and family and is an intelligent animal of extreme hardness and adaptability with a strong willingness to work, making her especially suitable as a companion, guardian, and general all-purpose dog.

OUR TRAINING EXPERIENCES

The Rottweiler is normally a rather independent dog, and this dog of cattle-driving origins has a bit of a stiff but absolutely honest character. She can be really stubborn at times, but at the same time is absolutely good-natured. If she's improperly raised, however, she can easily become out of control, especially if her fighting instincts and sharpness are increased through bad breeding and if in her upbringing she is not trained to develop psychological resistance to these instincts. In this somewhat late-blooming dog, the protection drive develops itself. The young dog has to learn to be subordinate to her people, and she should not become sharp too early. The Rottweiler needs a stable upbringing with clear consequences for misbehavior. The handler has to learn the special character of his or her dog, give her a task, and let her grow up in close contact with the family. A puppy with a stable character and normal social behavior will this way become a pleasant and trustworthy member of the family. If necessary, she will defend her family and their property, without, under normal circumstances, being a danger to other people. She usually is slower to learn than a shepherd dog, but what she learns she knows forever. The Rottweiler is a very fine dog for protection work, but not every handler is suitable for this type of dog.

Bouvier des Flandres

The Bouvier des Flandres (pronounced: Booviay duh Flawn-druh) is an ancient cattle dog that originates from the Belgian province of Flanders, which is situated along the North Sea coast in Belgium into the north of France. The Bouvier des Flandres (in Flemish: *Vlaanderse Veedrijver* or *Vlaamse Koehond*) has a grim countenance that is a result of her earlier work. She was originally bred and kept as a worker around farms, and she was a helper to cattle dealers. Her dark and stubborn expression helped her be a frightening guard of the farm and farmyard. Even today a Bouvier (this French word means "ox driver") is able to defend human, animal, hearth, and home, and her color, size, and hair structure underline this impression of strength.

At the beginning of the 20th century, Professor A. Reul, a researcher whose specialty was Belgian dog breeds, selected for building a specialized breed the somewhat heavy and squarely built Bouviers that he had found during his search for original Belgian dogs in the countryside. Two decades later, the Bouvier had a very good reputation and the breed became popular. A big difference between the contemporary Bouvier and the breed as it appeared at the beginning of the 20th century is the coat. The original Bouvier had a harsh coat, which had to be hand-stripped of dead hair to retain the proper texture. This coat was not as abundant (read: nice) as the much-softer coat of the modern, show-type Bouvier. The character of the Bouvier has also changed. It has, just like the coat, become much softer. Below we list the characteristics cited by the official breed standard, as well as characteristics we have noticed while training this breed.

GENERAL APPEARANCE

The Bouvier des Flandres is a powerfully built, compact, short-coupled, rough-coated dog of notably rugged appearance. She gives the impression of great strength without any sign of heaviness or clumsiness in her overall make-up. The head is impressive in scale, accentuated by a beard and mustache. The rough-coated ears are placed high and alert, and if cropped, the ears should be a triangular contour and in proportion to the size of the head. The inner corner of the ear should be in line with the outer corner of the eye. The tail formerly was docked, leaving two or three vertebrae. The tousled, double coat is luxuriant, with a dense mass of fine undercoat. The topcoat must be harsh to the touch, dry, trimmed, if necessary, to a length of approximately 2.5 inches (6 cm). All colors from fawn to black, passing through salt-and-pepper, gray and brindle are standard. The white- and the chocolate brown–colored coats, however, represent a serious fault.

The Bouvier des Flandres is a powerfully built, rough-coated dog.

SIZE

The height measured at the withers is for males 24.5 to 27.5 inches (62–68 cm)—the ideal is 26 inches (65 cm); for females the height is 23.5 to 26.5 inches (59–65 cm)—25 inches (62 cm) is the ideal.

CHARACTER

The Bouvier des Flandres is agile, spirited, and bold, yet her serene, well-behaved disposition denotes a steady, resolute, and fearless character. Her gaze is alert and brilliant, suggesting her intelligence, vigor, and daring. By nature, she is an equable dog.

OUR TRAINING EXPERIENCES

Bouviers are independent dogs that have a somewhat stiff character. They sometimes have the inclination to be strong-willed, which is especially manifested when one is teaching them to heel (on or off leash). In the beginning, it can be very difficult to get such dogs of cattle-driving origin to stay attentively beside their handlers. Of course, the personality of the handler plays a big role in this. To keep it interesting for a Bouvier, training has to be varied. The woolly and plump Bouvier puppy will grow to be a reasonably big, heavy, and strong dog that has to be educated in a logical way. The Bouvier is sometimes a slow study, but she remembers her lessons very well. Bouviers need a lot of movement and meaningful activity, which means owners need to devote time to them. Normally, Bouviers can live very well with all members of the family, including children and the family's cats. The steady, resolute, and fearless character mentioned in the breed standard has greatly decreased, however, as has her original willingness to work, which is why the number of Bouviers in training has gone down, although Bouviers really are fine dogs to train.

Giant Schnauzer

The giant schnauzer (in German: *Riesenschnauzer*) is a big dog whose ancestors were working dogs. They look something like shaved Bouviers, and there are certainly farm dogs and cattle dogs among their forebears. These farm dogs had spirit and sharpness and were watchful and devoted. Killing rats was their favorite activity, and it was beneficial to have them living with the horses in the stable. Originally the schnauzer (which means: "having a beard and mustache") was the dog of the stableman and wagoner, who preferred these big, powerful specimens with their wiry coats. The very abundant topcoat with the dense mass of fine undercoat kept the dogs warm during guard shifts near the wagons or the horses, and it protected them from rain. In the beginning, giant schnauzers were known as Munich schnauzers, but the name *Beer-schnauzer* was also sometimes used, because they guarded the cargo when beer wagons traveled from Munich into the countryside.

During World War I, other working characteristics of the breed were discovered. At the time, training schools for army and police dogs were established, and their shepherd and cattle-dog characteristics made schnauzers reliable in guarding and defense services as war dogs. At that time there were 60 giant schnauzers working in a German dog-training school in Berlin. The breed became a modern working dog, and 1925 it was officially qualified as a working breed in Germany. In 1936 the giant schnauzer Peter was given the title of "top working dog" of Germany, which meant that he was considered the best out of all the working breeds.

At this moment there are not many giant schnauzers taking part in police dog or Schutzhund training anymore, but that doesn't mean that they no longer have the right characteristics. Below we list the characteristics cited by the official breed standard, as well as characteristics we have noticed while training this breed.

GENERAL APPEARANCE

The giant schnauzer should resemble, as nearly as possible, a larger and more powerful version of the standard schnauzer, on the whole a bold and valiant figure of a dog: robust, strongly built, nearly square in proportion of body length to height at the withers, active, sturdy, and well-muscled. The sound, reliable temperament; rugged build; and dense, weather-resistant, wiry coat in solid black

The giant schnauzer has a weather-resistant, wiry coat that is solid black or salt-and-pepper in color.

or salt-and-pepper, make for one of the most useful, powerful, and enduring working breeds. The tail of the giant schnauzer formerly was docked to the second or not more than the third joint. If the ears are cropped, they are set high on the skull; when uncropped, the ears are V-shaped and carried rather high and close to the head.

SIZE
The height at the withers is between 23.5 and 27.5 inches (60–70 cm); males should be 25.5 to 27.5 inches (65–70 cm) and females 23.5 to 25.5 inches (60–65 cm). Medium heights in those ranges are preferred.

CHARACTER
The giant schnauzer's temperament combines spirit and alertness with intelligence and reliability. She is composed, watchful, courageous, easily trained, deeply loyal to family, playful, amiable in repose, and a commanding figure when aroused.

OUR TRAINING EXPERIENCES
Typical characteristics of the giant schnauzer are fearlessness in combination with deliberate calm and reliability. She has a good character and is absolutely loyal to her handler and family. Giant

schnauzers learn fast and normally get along well with children and other animal members of the family. She is a devoted dog that likes to work for her handler, but she can be stubborn in the face of a tough approach to training. Many giant schnauzers like to be cuddled, but this inclination doesn't preclude them from having good working-dog characteristics.

Doberman

The Doberman is well-known all over the world. The breed came into being about 150 years ago in the German province of Thüringen, around the capital city of Apolda. The breed was created by Friedrich Louis Dobermann (1836–94), who wanted to create a dog with strong protection and guard qualities. The Doberman owes her nice outlook and versatile mental characteristics to a medley of all sorts of dogs. To begin, Louis Dobermann searched for dogs with courage and sharpness to contribute to his courageous breed. Louis Dobermann himself could use such dogs because he fulfilled, among other professions such as dog catcher, the functions of tax collector and night watchman. He needed a dog to protect him and one that would "encourage" slow taxpayers. At that time, his creation was nicknamed the "gendarme dog." Since then, the old gendarme dog has developed into an aristocratic athlete with many useful qualities. This change from a defense dog into an all-round working dog is a result of the interference of breeders who, after the death of Louis Dobermann, busied themselves to "perfect" the breed. The Doberman is still a very good working dog, and she performs a variety of tasks in countries the world over. In some movies this breed is, absolutely contrary the truth, portrayed as a bloodthirsty fighting machine. Below we list the characteristics cited by the official breed standard, as well as characteristics we have noticed while training this breed.

GENERAL APPEARANCE

The appearance is that of dog of medium size, with a body that is square. The Doberman is compactly built, muscular and

Like the German shepherd dog, the Doberman is also well-known the world over.

powerful, and capable of great endurance and speed. She is elegant in appearance, with a proud carriage reflecting great nobility and a fine temperament.

SIZE

The height at the withers for males is between 26 and 28 inches (68–72 cm), and the ideal is about 27.5 inches (70 cm); females should be 24 to 26 inches (63–68 cm), with their ideal height being about 25.5 inches (65 cm).

CHARACTER

Dobermans are energetic, watchful, determined, alert, fearless, loyal, and obedient.

OUR TRAINING EXPERIENCES

A good Doberman has, according to the breed standard, a medium temperament, a medium sharpness, and a medium prickle threshold. With a good Doberman that is willing to work, the handler has to be attentive to the pressure to achieve, as well as the dog's courage and toughness. The dog should be given a high level of self-confidence and fearlessness with respect to her surroundings. Most Dobermans are high-spirited dogs that react quickly to all sorts of things in their surroundings (people, objects, animals). As with all watchful dogs, they can sometimes be a bit "barky"; unnecessary barking has to be curtailed. Remember that a self-confident dog doesn't have to bark immediately when something happens in her surroundings. She will first watch developments attentively, and only when she perceives that there is danger does she become active. The self-confident dog knows, for sure, that she can manage the situation.

A certain sharpness in Dobermans isn't a problem, but the dog shouldn't also be frightened or nervous. A low prickle threshold can, in combination with frightening situations, become a problem. Toughness is the dog's ability to recover after a negative experience. An extremely tough dog cannot be corrected, and for sure not by tough corrections, because such corrections don't impress her. A soft approach to a dog with a tendency to toughness often has a surprising effect; she doesn't expect gentleness and so reacts in the correct way.

The Doberman is a reliable pet, but she will not fit every family. Dobermans normally are good mates with the children of the family. If games get a little too wild and a scratch results on the child's arm or leg, it is just an accident and not a sign of unreliable behavior. Assuming that a Doberman puppy is bred correctly and has stable parents, her career as a protection dog will particularly be determined by her education. She is smart, and that sounds attractive, but it also means she will remember everything, even your inconsistencies, and if it suits her, she will manipulate you. What you want, or don't want, has to be an iron law for the puppy or young dog. Furthermore, the Doberman is an active dog. She enjoys all forms of activity, variety, and challenge. In training, the Doberman is a lively and enthusiastic dog that normally walks in an agile way with her handler in the obedience exercises and works out the given commands quickly and spontaneously. With decoy work, the bite of Dobermans is sometimes a bit restless, which means the dog bites, shortly outs, and then bites again several times, or as trainers say, "plays piano." Besides that, a Doberman can sometimes spontaneously run riot, often even leaving the training field. After a short time, she will come back with an amazed look in her eyes, happily running toward her desperate handler.

Boxer

In the Middle Ages in Europe, a theory developed that the meat of a calm or placid cow or bull would be tough and not fit to eat. That's why cattle, shortly before the slaughter, were stirred up, so the meat would be bloodier and therefore tastier. For that reason, butchers employed big, heavy dogs whose job it was to tease and excite the animals before the axe fell. Later on, some people began to breed a smaller and more maneuverable dog, the so-called "bull biter." These dogs were also used as guard dogs, but they were gentle with their owners and the family. These dogs were allowed to come into the house and took part in family life. Soon, especially in southern Germany, the name "boxer" was used for these dogs. In the beginning of 1890 in Munich, someone began a plan to breed boxers. The idea was to create a dog that combined mass, beauty, and correct behavior. The dog had to jump like a cat, but she also had to attack and defend like a mastiff. At first sight, these characteristics look contradictory, but looking at the modern boxer, we have to agree that a lot of these wishes have been fulfilled.

The boxer is tremendously popular in a lot of European countries and the United States. During World War II, boxers were employed in war duties such as guarding and patrolling. The breed was not damaged by the violence of the war. After that period, the boxer's popularity around the world soared, and her many abilities were made use of. Most boxers today are reliable pets. They are fond of children, pleasant, obedient, and clever, and they are almost always ready to play. Boxers trained as Schutzhunds or protection dogs maintain that "good pet" character. Below we list the characteristics cited by the official breed standard, as well as characteristics we have noticed while training this breed.

GENERAL APPEARANCE

The ideal boxer is a medium-sized, square-built dog of good substance with a short back, strong limbs, and short, tight-fitting coat. Her well-developed muscles are clean, hard, and appear smooth under taut skin. Her movements denote energy. The gait is firm, yet elastic, the stride free and ground-covering, the carriage proud. Developed to serve as a guard, working, and companion dog, she combines strength and agility with elegance and style. Her expression is alert and temperament steadfast and tractable. If cropped, the ears are cut rather long and tapering, raised when alert; uncropped ears should be carried close to the head. The coat colors are fawn and brindle. White markings may not exceed one-third of the entire coat.

SIZE

Adult males are 22.5 to 25 inches (57–63 cm) at the withers, and females are 21 to 23.5 inches (53–59 cm).

CHARACTER

Character is of paramount importance in the boxer. Instinctively a "hearing" guard dog, her bearing is alert, dignified, and self-assured.

The boxer is a medium-sized, square-built dog with a short, tight-fitting coat.

With family and friends, her temperament is fundamentally playful, yet she is patient and stoic with children. Deliberate and wary with strangers, she will exhibit curiosity, but she shows fearless courage if threatened. However, she responds promptly to friendly overtures honestly rendered. Her intelligence, loyal affection, and tractability to discipline make her a highly desirable companion.

OUR TRAINING EXPERIENCES

With her short nose, the boxer sometimes has difficulties with breathing, in particular during bouts of extreme warmth and great effort. Normally, she is friendly with people, but she is sometimes less tolerant with other animals. She has to be raised with clear consequences for her actions to prevent her from misbehaving in the house and with other dogs. The boxer is lively and jumpy, likes to play, and can be used for many purposes. Training, however, has to be varied to maintain her enthusiasm and willingness to work. Because of incorrect training with too much pressure, many boxers give the impression that they work because they have to, not happily. A lot of variety and enough time to play are important to her training. Boxers have a pleasant and trustful character. Deterrence of unwanted visitors is usually not their priority, but if necessary they will defend their family and properties. They aren't afraid in dangerous situations or frightened of pain. Boxers can very easily learn a lot, and it makes sense for us to employ their power and defensive characters in Schutzhund or protection dog training. We must emphasize that boxers are excellent and reliable biters in decoy work. It's a pity that we don't see them very much on the training field.

Airedale Terrier

This breed originated in the middle of the 19th century in England from mixes of different breeds. The first part of the dog's name comes from the valley of the Aire, a small river in the county of Yorkshire, where the breed originally worked as an otter hunter. The word "terrier" is derived from the Latin *terra* (earth) and relates to the work these dogs do in hunting badgers and foxes under the ground. In general, small terriers were employed to hunt these animals, but small terriers were too little and lightly built for hunting otters. The otter is a dangerous opponent, enticing his opponent into the water to drown him, so otter hunting needs more powerful dogs. The otter hound, which was also used for this hunt, was missing the typical terrier characteristics: spiritedness, cockiness, confidence, and sometimes combativeness and courageousness. So, the right dog for the job was created by breeding: mixing the fierceness of terriers with the size of otter hounds, as well as the otter hound's firm, waterproof coat, suitable for going into the water. In the beginning, these mixes were called "waterside" or "working" terriers. Later on, however, the breed received, because of its size and dignified character, the title King of the Terriers. In the United States, hunters made grateful use of the Airedale terrier's character in bear hunting, while in France she was used to hunt wild boar. The Airedale terrier can be called an all-round working dog; in addition to being a great hunter, she has also won her spurs as a police, defense, and army dog.

The Airedale terrier adapts easily to different circumstances and can be kept in almost every situation. Although she bears the spry and fiery character of a terrier, she can be called the most self-restrained of all terriers. The Airedale terrier differs from other terriers in her dignity and stateliness, and she is not as quick-tempered as most other terriers. Sometimes she can be fierce with small game (and cats), but normally she is friendly to people and pleasant with children. In spite of her friendly character, the Airedale terrier will not hesitate to defend her handler or the family. Below we list the characteristics cited by the official breed standard, as well as characteristics we have noticed while training this breed.

GENERAL APPEARANCE

Largest of the terriers, the Airedale is a muscular, active, fairly cobby dog, without suspicion of legginess or undue length of body. Both sexes should be sturdy, well-muscled and -boned. The ears should be V-shaped with carriage to the side of the head, small, but not out of proportion to the size of the dog. The coat should be hard, dense, and wiry, lying straight and close, covering the dog well over the body and legs. Some of the hardest coats are crinkling or just slightly waved. The head and ears should be tan, the ears being a darker shade than the rest of the body. The legs up to the thighs and elbows and the under part of the body and chest are also tan, and the tan color frequently runs into the shoulder. The sides and upper parts of the body should be black or dark grizzle. A small white blaze on the chest is a characteristic of certain strains of the breed.

The Airedale
terrier has a hard
and wiry coat.

SIZE

Males should measure approximately 23 inches (58–61 cm) in height at the shoulder; females should measure slightly less, between 22 and 23 inches (56 and 59 cm).

CHARACTER

The Airedale terrier is keen of expression, quick of movement, and on the tiptoe of expectation at any movement. Her character is denoted and shown by the expression of her eyes, and by the carriage of her ears and erect tail. Her temperament is outgoing and confident, friendly, courageous, and intelligent. She is alert at all times, not aggressive but fearless.

OUR TRAINING EXPERIENCES

The Airedale terrier is an easy dog that can be raised without many problems to be an obedient working dog. You have to take her passion for hunting into account, but if you offer her an appealing alternative to the hunt, she won't give you any difficulties. Provided she gets plenty of outside time and space for playing and living it up, one could almost forget her presence in the house, she is so quiet. She likes to lie at the feet of her owner and waits quietly for him or her to return when away. Outside, she is a happy, frisky dog and an Airedale will play until an advanced age. She is pleasant and affectionate, and although she will not learn as quickly as most shepherd dogs, she can be taught everything and is employable in many ways. The Airedale terriers we see in training are really a feast for the eyes. Energetic, full of temperament, and very attentive, they keep an eye on their handlers, so they can immediately follow all their movements. These quiet and pretty working dogs also show what they are made of in defense work. It is wonderful to see these dogs at work with decoys: their enthusiasm and willingness to work makes many trainers' mouths water. The Airedale terrier has courage and is alert, has a keen expression and a particular good ability to react. Like the boxer, however—and more's the pity—we don't see them very often in training.

The Dutch KNPV Dogs

Unlike dog sport programs such as IPO, Schutzhund, and even French Ring, the Royal Dutch Police Dog Association (*Koninklijke Nederlandse Politiehond Vereniging*, or KNPV) has no requirement for their dogs to hold an official pedigree. In fact, around about 90 per cent of the dogs titled in the KNPV program do not have official pedigrees. The KNPV believes that official pedigrees are not required to produce quality police dogs, and the continuing success of the program and its organization has proven this to be true.

The KNPV was originally formed as the NPV on November 1, 1907, in a town called Roosendaal in Noord-Brabant, the Netherlands. The "K" *Koninklijke* (Royal) was not added until February 28, 1912. At this point, police dog training already had a history in the Netherlands. In those days, when people talked about a police dog, they mostly thought of the qualities of the dog's nose, qualities that sadly were highly overestimated. The dog's abilities to bite and hear were more or less overlooked, but soon it was clear that these protection qualities of police dogs were very important for police work, too. The first trial rules were made in 1908, but many additions and changes followed, dictated by experience with the dogs and the development of realistic expectations. One rule that never changed, however, was that a dog had to be totally controllable at all times in order to pass.

In the early days, even before the (K)NPV was founded, various breeds and cross-breeds were used for police work in the Netherlands. In the first 25 years of the organization's existence, a limited number of dogs received a KNPV title, not quite 33 dogs a year, the low being 1921 with 12 dogs and the high in 1925 with 60. Today approximately one thousand certificates in the combined disciplines are issued every year.

The dogs that were used most in the early days were German shepherds, Dutch shepherds, Dobermans, Belgian Malinois, Tervuren, Groenendaels (Belgian sheepdogs), and Bouviers. The

German shepherd was popular in the KNPV of that time, probably because people used the dogs that were readily available to them.

Due to the breeding policy for the Dutch shepherds, dictated by the official Dutch shepherd breeding club (NHC), a lot of good dogs were excluded as Dutch shepherds (e.g., in 1914, suddenly only brindle dogs could be registered, whereas up to that point, many colors, including "yellow," had been permitted), but these same dogs could be entered as Belgian Malinois in those days. This may explain part of the sudden increase of Malinois in the KNPV at the time.

At this point, too, the breeding of dogs of unknown background started to happen more and more. This was partly because of finances (crosses were cheaper than pedigreed dogs) and partly because the Dutch Kennel Club, Raad van Beheer op Kynologisch Gebied in Nederland, contrary to surrounding countries, did not require dogs to have a working title of some kind to win a championship in conformation.

Thus we can, as early as 1932, hear the complaint that pedigreed dogs with a correct temperament for KNPV work were few and far between. Later, after World War II in particular, due to financial constraints, many puppies of pedigreed litters were not registered with the FCI. This was simply because registering cost money and people felt that a simple piece of paper would not make their dog a better one. The split between pedigreed and non-pedigreed dogs was thus created, and even today the majority of KNPV dogs are not FCI registered, which does not necessarily mean that the lineage of these dogs is unknown. Today most breeders are fully aware of working lines within the KNPV, and most dogs—pedigreed or not—share some very solid working lines that go back a long way.

X DUTCH SHEPHERDS (XHH)

Today there are considered to be two types of Dutch shepherd (in Dutch: *Hollandse Herder*). The first is the FCI-registered Dutch shepherd. This dog is bred to FCI standards with official pedigree and generally competes in conformation shows or is trained in various dog sports and working pursuits such as IPO, agility, obedience, and search and rescue (SAR). These dogs, like most pedigreed dogs, are mainly bred for conformation showing as per FCI standards, with only a few breeders concentrating on producing dogs specifically for working pursuits. The registered Dutch shepherd is not a large breed in terms of numbers, with approximately four thousand dogs currently registered.

The second type of Dutch shepherd is that most commonly found in the KNPV training programs. In the Netherlands the unregistered Dutch shepherd (xHH, where x stands for cross bred *Hollandse Herder*) is one of the mainstay breeds of police dog training, along with the ever-popular Malinois. Within the KNPV program, the Dutch shepherd has survived without the influence and pressures of the conformation circles and has not been restricted by the need for an official pedigree. The xHH is, and always has been, bred to be a working police dog. Even within the KNPV program, however, the Dutch shepherd is still relatively small in population compared to the Malinois, yet it continues to maintain a working police dog heritage that few breeds can match.

The xHH dogs found in the KNPV training have a strong influence of Malinois blood in them. Without the restriction of official registration or pedigree, the definition of whether a dog is a Malinois or a Dutch shepherd primarily comes down to appearance. When a Malinois is bred to a Dutch shepherd, some of the pups will be born with a fawn coat and will be known as unregistered Malinois (xMH); others will be born with a brindle coat and will be known as unregistered Dutch shepherds. This simple classification process has allowed the xHH (and xMH, for that matter) to develop and maintain a large gene pool for breeding. Although the xHH can carry a good deal of Malinois blood, people often comment that they still maintain the desirable traits

The mixed Dutch shepherd (xHH) is one of the mainstay breeds
of police dog training in the Netherlands.

of the Dutch shepherd: a highly driven, sometimes stubborn dog
with more calmness than a Malinois. In general, the xHH is a
large dog (males can reach over 27.5 inches [70 cm] at the shoulder and weigh up to 121 pounds [55 kg], while females can reach
over 25.5 inches [65 cm] and weigh up to 88 pounds [40 kg]),
with larger bones and head size than officially registered dogs.
They also commonly have a far more highly and widely regarded
working character than the Dutch shepherds bred solely to official
breed standards.

The search for quality working dogs for police, military, and
high-level competition around the world has led to a large demand
for the xHH, and as such this breed will become a far more common sight in different service departments around the world, just
as it has in its Dutch homeland. And although these dogs often
have a good deal of Belgian Malinois blood in them, it is amazing
how their characters always include that of the typically intelligent, stubborn, handler-oriented *Herder*.

X BELGIAN MALINOIS (XMH)

In the IPO, agility, obedience, and SAR training programs, registered Malinois are seen much more often than unregistered

The mixed Malinois (xMH) has proven its value in the KNPV police dog training program.

Malinois (xMH, where x stands for cross-bred *Mechelse Herder*). The xMH are very rare because of the official international cynological rules that only allow Malinois with pedigree in championships.

Belgium, Holland, and France are the countries where this breed was developed as an outstanding working dog, not only for sporting but also as a practical police and patrol dog. The character of the xMH is to be classified as full of temperament but also stable and social in interaction with people, a characteristic that cannot be ascribed to many other modern breeds.

The history of the Malinois in the Netherlands compared to the Malinois in France is very different. Only registered Malinois were bred in France, while the Netherlands is the only country where mixed Malinois (xMH) were also bred. In the 20th century, the xMH was more used than the registered one, especially within the KNPV and the professional sector. One of the reasons for this was the awkward financial position of the European dog handler directly after World War II. Money had to be spent on daily needs. Everything had to be as inexpensive as possible, and people did not make room for the expense associated with registering pedigrees, even if both parent dogs were pedigreed. Another reason for the rise of the xMH is the culture of the KNPV training program, where handlers did not see any extra value to using registered Malinois.

Today the xMH has proven its value in the KNPV program, although more registered Malinois have been appearing on the police dog training fields.

3

Training Methods

Many handlers wear themselves out at the training fields trying to teach dogs certain exercises. Sometimes they drill for months, but very often the result is that not even the slightest progress is made or even that the dog resists the exercise. Often you notice that the training method used simply doesn't capture the dog's interest. Why not choose a method that fits the dog instead of working for months to fit the dog to the method? Typically, handlers take no account of their dog's character when planning a training schedule. The education of a young dog must never be superficial. It should not be limited to a few obedience exercises. A proper upbringing should stimulate all the good and useful characteristics that lie dormant in young dogs. At the same time, we have to avoid stirring up undesirable habits.

Mechanical Training

If we really want to bring the dog to a full development of her possibilities, training always must be focused on the dog's nature and characteristics. Mechanical training is never optimal and frustrates both humans and dogs. On a lot of training fields, however, training is conducted in a mechanical fashion, partly out of ignorance and partly because of a so-called lack of time. An example of mechanical training would be the following methods of teaching the dog to sit: We push on the dog's rear with one hand, pull the leash upward diagonally with the other hand, and at the same time we give the command "Sit." For that, the handler needs no knowledge of dogs but only the directives from the instructor. Humans in a hurry still use this method, without worrying about their dogs. They believe dogs have to be trained as fast as possible, but in doing so they neglect to build the foundation to all good training: a strong bond between handler and dog. That this type of mechanical training is still used on too many training fields shows a great lack of knowledge and understanding of dogs. Remember that training time can be viewed as a pleasant hobby for both humans and dogs. Dogs have to be developed very carefully; we should never worry about time in this regard.

Mechanical training uses pressure and physical preponderance. By our physical power the dog is forced to do what we demand. The philosophy behind this kind of training is the opposite of the one we espouse, in which humans must do a lot of work to understand their dogs before and during training. Think about it. We can take the dog far by understanding and out-thinking her. We can allow her to perform with pleasure that which we want her to do. Those who try to train a dog using violence always give themselves a *testimonium paupertatis*, a testament to their own mental poverty.

The chosen training method obviously suits this Dutch shepherd dog.

Learning through Play

Handlers have to be convinced to allow their dogs to work more in line with the dogs' characteristics, their individuality. Modern dog training demands that humans study this individuality that also prevents us from using predictable, boring patterns to train our dogs.

People are often convinced that the opposite of mechanical training—and thus the best method—is the so-called "learning through play" strategy by which the dog learns only by playing. This method, however, is ineffective and not realistic. Dogs trained for personal protection must learn how to do many tasks that play simply will not address; in order for dogs to learn how to do these things properly, we sometimes need to apply a certain amount of pressure. We have heard people suggest that their dogs do certain exercises "all by themselves," but such dogs typically only perform when it suits them and not always when we want them to.

Voluntarily performed exercises, however, underscore the natural characteristics of the dog, or her natural tendency to behave in a particular way. It would be stupid not to employ these characteristics in training. It would, however, be much more stupid to punish a dog for her natural tendencies, so that the drive to perform the tasks she loves fades away, and then later on we have to force the dog to perform them.

"Ridiculous," you may think. "That wouldn't happen." If only you could see how many times we have seen young dogs punished for carrying sticks and other articles, and then later on in training these same dogs had to learn to retrieve. Or how many young dogs have not been allowed to sniff at everything they encounter, but later on have to be taught tracking and scent-discrimination.

Individual Characteristics

Training that takes the dog's nature into account makes good use of the inherited abilities of dogs. When the play drive of the dog is encouraged at the same time, this has little or nothing to do with free playing (see the "learning through play" method above). This kind of structured playing allows the dog to stay under the influence of our intentions. As well, the manner of training ensures that the dog almost never becomes uncomfortable while learning the exercises. Because of that, she will always work cheerfully, and she will learn and work out the exercises with great reliability. Besides, such a way of training is a lot more pleasant and inspiring for the handler.

Of course, there is a big difference between training that takes the dog's nature into account and mechanical training, which relies on performance of certain acts or rituals. By taking the dog's

Training that takes your dog's individual nature into account makes good use of her inherited abilities.

character into account, we use our brains instead of our brawn to train our dogs. Mechanical training often employs a great deal of rough, physical violence. When we work with our dogs, we don't need to be rough. This type of training that considers individual character does not only apply to obedience training but also to any follow-up training you may wish to engage in. Our working dogs, including protection dogs, must be obedient, reliable, tough, and courageous. Thus, a protection dog's upbringing should be focused from the beginning on bringing out these traits, which are required in so many exercises.

Benefits of Training Early

Many people ask us, "When should we start training?" The answer: As early as possible, even with an eight-week-old puppy. Early training is interesting for the dog as well as for people, and it yields good results. Besides, the attention received and movement engaged in early exercises will contribute to the young dog's development. Also, dogs' lives are short; when you start working with your dog early, you ensure that you and your dog will enjoy one another's company for as long as possible. Working with your dog is good for your health and that of your dog, because you must both spend a lot of time out in the fresh air and engage in a lot of exercise.

Note that if you have children, dog training can bring with it an extra advantage. The traits and awareness we demand from a dog in training are also very important in the education of children: self-control, tranquility, deliberation, stamina, perseverance, patience, willpower, justice, and social structure. The proper training and handling of dogs therefore also has a very good influence on the education of our children.

The Intelligent Dog

How much do we consider the dog's mind and her thinking ability when it comes to her education and training? This a frequently asked question, which can be of great importance in determining the successful completion of training. Dogs' instinct, memory, and intelligence have been hot topics of discussion for years. Regarding instinct, it is agreed that the way dogs act cannot be based only on instinct. It is clear that dogs must also have a good working memory. Sometimes you hear that dogs act on the basis of instinct coupled with memory. But some behavioral scientists, ethnologists, are not satisfied with that explanation of dog behavior. They demonstrate that the dog also possesses a form of intellect. Of course, there are scientists who disagree, which in turn creates confusion for the rest of us.

Dog handlers and trainers need a training method that employs both our own observations of dogs and the "facts" that science produces. It is especially important that we not under- or overestimate the mental skills of our dogs. To clarify a picture of the mental skills of the dog, we discuss what we mean by instinct, memory, and intellect below.

INSTINCT, MEMORY, AND INTELLECT

By *instinct*, we mean the inherent mechanism of behavior that appears in a certain fixed sequence of movements and the outcome of those movements. An instinct is a natural drive that is carried out involuntarily, such as the drive for food acquisition and the drive for reproduction.

To fully develop your dog's potential, training should always be geared to her particular characteristics.

By *memory*, we mean action without awareness or acting involuntarily in the right way on the basis of collected memories. Scientists call these kinds of memories "associations." For instance, the dog connects certain words (commands) with a particular exercise that she has to perform. As soon as she hears the word, she remembers the associated exercise and works out the steps to perform it without being aware of what she is doing.

By *intellect*, we mean everything that goes further than instinct and memory, like acting with awareness or the capacity for logical thinking. The goal of the act is recognized before conclusions or decisions are made to work toward that goal. Many people (not we) deny the dog has this capacity.

THE MEMORY/INTELLECT CONNECTION

In the "psychological view" of dog training, it is said that a dog only can learn to do something unpleasant when she is forced to by the pressure to keep something more unpleasant from happening. For instance, if the dog doesn't like lying down on command, you can force her to lie down by using a prick collar or jerking on the leash, and she will do it to avoid the prick collar or the jerking. This theory also postulates that the dog's actions are linked solely to her memories.

But isn't memory the seed of much thought? Indeed, if we can remember something, then we can imagine it. That's not so different from thinking. In dog training, the faculty of memory, or acting on what memory is "telling" the dog to do, plays a big role. Some exercises definitely indicate that memory is at work, for instance, the exercises Sit and Down. With these, the dog works out the command using instinct and memory only, because these exercises are done in fractions of seconds.

However, if you are teaching your dog to search, something more than instinct and memory comes into play. Take the following hypothetical situation, for example. You throw an article far out, into high grass, and then give the command "Search." Your dog hears the command but doesn't see where the article is. Also, a tail wind isn't bringing the odor to her nose. So, your dog searches for about five minutes in the grass, then locates the article and retrieves it. This five-minute search cannot be seen as an unconscious act. The dog had to think continuously about the command she had been given and how to execute her duty for five minutes straight. Without thinking, performing this task would have been impossible for her.

In determining the intelligence of dogs, however, we should not limit our observations to the training field. This is an unsuitable location for such assessments because here dogs are constantly under pressure and cannot simply be themselves; on the field, we don't see who the individual dog really is and what she wants. The still much-too-often-used mechanical training stifles all the dog's independent, conscious acts and her mental development. We cannot emphasize enough that mechanical training is not the best for dogs or people—engaging in such training transforms a dog into a living machine, a robot that moves when the right button is switched on. We have to change our methods from "train" to "educate," and then we will see our dogs' intellect shine through.

Observing a dog that is free of pressure, we often see the dog act in an aware, well-considered, logical way. A dog that wants to play "fetch" will, "without encouragement," drop an object at her handler's feet. She will then give unmistakable signals to encourage the handler to throw the object so she can pick it up again. These actions do not demonstrate instinct and memory alone. No, the dog that wants to play in this way is demonstrating intellect; she is aware and focused on acting to achieve a goal. She is thinking. And what of the dog that is separated from her handler and refuses food for many days? Wouldn't such sadness be due to memories of her handler, thoughts about the handler?

Memory and intellect are such closely connected concepts that they can't be separated. If dogs have memory, then they have intellect. Of course, there is a big difference between the intellect of a dog and that of a human, and we have to keep this in mind when

Dog training, like this exercise of jumping over a ditch, should always be a pleasure for your dog and you, the handler.

we train dogs. We cannot expect a dog to think like a human. However, should we claim the dog has no intellect and try to train her with that understanding, we'll have to train her using forceful, mechanical methods, breaking her will. The successful method that takes the dog's character—and intellect—into account, however, proves that we can train dogs in a much better way.

Someone who doesn't believe dogs think, who can only train them by the principle that a dog performs something unpleasant to prevent something even more unpleasant, will not succeed in training his or her dog as a protection dog. A dog that has to *revier* (search for the odor of hidden persons or dangerous objects) has to think, or she will not succeed. Dogs can learn to search for odors and hidden persons; they can sustain thoughts to execute complex tasks. Therefore, dogs can think.

4

Our Relationship with Dogs

How we associate with dogs as we raise and train them, and how we speak commands, is important. A lot of people set great store by commands spoken in a short, military way. Obviously, this manner shows that one has power over the dog. On the other hand, some people speak much too softly. If we teach a dog an exercise, the command should be spoken clearly and in a friendly tone; it has to be spoken not too loud but also not too soft. A louder than normal command will represent a reprimand to the dog. Too-loud commands often make the dog contrary, inattentive, and numb. If the dog is well-versed in the exercises, it is possible to give the commands in a softer tone, which gets the dog's attention. A dog that quickly and correctly responds to the softest commands, or even to the smallest signals, shows that she and her handler understand each other well.

The tone in which commands are given must suit the exercise. Depending on the situation and the exercise, the commands sometimes must be spoken in an encouraging, reassuring, or praising tone, perhaps drawn out or, alternatively, clipped. You should only use one command for each particular exercise. We may not like having someone tell us which commands we must use to train our dogs, but if we are training for a certain diploma at an examination, certain commands may be required. Using the dog's name with

The commands and the tone in which they are given must fit the type of exercise you and your dog are working on.

the command is sometimes also allowed. We have to ensure that we always use a particular, chosen command for the same exercise. Dogs are certainly able to recall more than one command, but we must not make training more difficult for the dog than it already is. Later on, we can substitute signals or normal speech for commands to get the dog to perform every exercise she has already been taught.

Praise

When raising a dog, it's important to understand when to reward and when to punish. When praising your dog, don't limit yourself to single words or phrases. Praising is not like giving commands. We can praise in various ways: "That's a good girl, well done, that's correct." The characteristic words for the reward are, indeed, "Good girl" (or "Good boy"), but by using more words, we can clearly tell our dogs that they have done well. In dog training, much depends on the correct reward given, and the way the dog understands the reward.

If your dog shows that she doesn't understand a certain exercise, simplify the exercise by breaking it down into steps, for instance. As soon as she begins the exercise—it is too late when she already has worked out the exercise—praise her in a cheerful and encouraging

Praise and encouragement stimulate the dog's performance of the exercise.

way. You will see that your dog will come to understand the exercise better that way, which helps both of you avoid frustration and confusion. For a lot of people, it is difficult to offer cheerful praise when they are actually disappointed and dissatisfied with their dogs. But having complete control of your feelings is one of the most important characteristics required in dog training. Remember, your dog will quickly figure out if you're not sincere. If you can't control your inner feelings and the manifestation of those feelings, the sound of your disappointment will come out in your praise, and your dog will lose confidence in your praise and become less motivated.

Reprimand

The opposite of praise is the reprimand. While we express our satisfaction by praising the dog, we show her our displeasure with a reprimand. The reprimand, just like the reward, is not a command. For praising we normally use the words "Good girl" (or a variation of that), and for a reprimand it's a good idea to use the softly spoken "Uh, uh" (pronounced "əh, əh"). Ensure you use a disappointed tone when saying "Uh, uh."

Generally the word "No" is used for a reprimand, but that's a mistake, because "No" is also a condemnation, a punishment for something that is not allowed. It is a good thing to clearly differentiate between a reprimand and a condemnation or punishment. Your dog will hear a reprimand when she makes a mistake in training an exercise. If she's doing something that she's forbidden to do, she will recognize it as a strong condemnation of that behavior. For instance, if your dog knows how to retrieve and then drops a retrieving dumbbell, she will be reprimanded—"Uh, uh" here translates as: "Eh, what is this? Bring me the dumbbell!"

But when she does something that's not allowed, for instance, picking up and eating something off the ground, then you must utter a powerful "No." The harshly spoken "No" means that she immediately has to stop what she is doing. "No" has to work as a lash; it has to mean that the dog must not do whatever she is doing ever again. So, it is contradictory to use "No" as a reprimand for a badly worked-out exercise. Indeed, the dog may not make this mistake again, but she still has to work out that exercise!

In receiving the reprimand "No" for mistakes in training, the dog may think two things, or both: "No" is meant for the whole exercise and so she therefore is not allowed to perform that exercise; or "No" has been spoken as a punishment for forbidden behavior, and the word will become less and less effective the more often it is used for both reprimand and punishment.

The dog must ignore commands given by the decoy, like "Out," or "Go away."

Punishment

When, how, and with what should you punish your dog? These are three important questions, to which the answers are of the utmost importance for success in raising and training dogs. One single punishment at the wrong moment, a too-heavy punishment or one administered with the wrong article, can totally upset a months' long, laborious training period. The dog has to experience a correct punishment for it to be effective.

When do we have to punish? When she breaks a rule, your dog should be punished at the moment of the offense. If some time (even seconds) has already passed, your dog may not be aware that she has even done anything wrong. As well, some dogs should be punished for some mistakes made in training, especially when such mistakes can lead to serious problems. As we discuss the exercises later in this book, we will also discuss when punishment is appropriate.

How should you punish? Briefly, but in a way that's clear for the dog. The dog learns nothing from weak punishment, and this leads to endless repetition. As a matter of fact, how tough your punishments are depends on your dog. A tough, obstinate dog has to be dealt with more strongly than a sensitive dog. You should also take the dog's age into account and whether or not the dog knew her behavior was not allowed when deciding on the seriousness of the punishment.

The first degree of punishment is a sharp and loud "No"; the second is a rap with the hand, and, if necessary, we have to give a tougher punishment. However, never allow your anger to color how you perceive your dog's offense. Remember that punishment helps a dog to learn something—it should not be a vehicle for your anger. If your dog is caught in the act, it isn't necessary to put her on leash before you punish her. It weakens the punishment if you wait to put your dog on leash before acting. Punishing during the act will normally be a harsh "No" and/or a short, clear rap.

Punish with What?

We always punish a dog with our voice. But what can you use on a stubborn dog if the voice doesn't work? The discussion has been ongoing for many years. One side suggests using a rolled-up newspaper, while another side argues that your hand is most effective. We agree with the latter. When you take a rolled-up newspaper with you wherever you go, the dog sees it and doesn't make mistakes. However, if you forget to take the newspaper, it is not possible to punish the dog properly. You always have your hand with you. Of course, you should never hit your dog impetuously, but a swift tap can be necessary for some obstinate dogs.

Punishment with a stick, whip, or something else is absolutely incorrect, and the same goes for kicking. Punishment with the wrong article can undermine training. For instance, if a dog doesn't want to hold the dumbbell, and you tap her head with it, you can be sure she will never again hold that dumbbell. Punishment with a chain collar can be effective when you are heeling on leash. When the dog doesn't walk correctly, a short, strong jerk on the leash will make it clear that this is not allowed. For punishment at a distance, we can also throw a chain collar toward the dog. But never throw it at the dog, only toward her immediate surroundings. Such punishment should always be combined with "No," so later on just "No" is enough.

Some people use electronic training collars that dole out punishment or "correction" with electric shocks, euphemistically described as "weak current." These are absolutely reprehensible tools, which are sadly used more and more. They are often used by impatient handlers or instructors who want to see fast results or by people who aren't able to train dogs in another way. Many studies prove that, in humans as well as in other animals, even "harmless" electric shocks can cause serious changes in muscular tissue, particularly the heart muscle, and damage to brain tissue. These changes range from minor bleeding to irreparable tissue damage. It is scandalous to use such devices on any creature.

Temptations

Normally it isn't necessary to train dogs in a closed room. Most of the time, dog training takes place in the open air, in a place where there is little or no traffic. Dogs easily get used to all sorts of disturbances in nature. As their education and training progress, dogs can work under increasingly more distracting circumstances. Other dogs and helpers on the training field, female dogs in heat, cats, birds, game, a lot of people talking, and children playing should not be obstacles for the dog to continue her training, at least, not if the training offers the dog enough variety.

Remember, it is not necessary to follow the sequence of the exercises as described in some books. Many exercises can be trained separately, which allows you to offer a lot more variety than that of a fixed program that often causes the handler and dog to lose interest and therefore concentration. Exercises such as Heel, Retrieve, Bark on Command, and the Long Down Under Distraction are not connected, so training for them can occur in any order. But exercises that are connected, such as Heel on Leash and Heel off Leash, have to be trained in the right sequence. The last exercise is only trained when the dog walks correctly on leash.

Working Out the Exercises

Never train for too long at a time, and don't train the same exercise for too long. When training is pleasant and interesting for the dog, you will have fun, too. An exercise may be repeated about three or four times. However, usually one discovers that even this is too often. The dog's attention wavers, and because of that the exercise will be worked out badly. Then you, the handler, become irritated, and that will have further consequences for your dog, which then works even worse. In this way, the downward spiral, which so often makes dog training difficult and unpleasant, begins.

That's why it is much better to work out a difficult exercise at the beginning of a training session and immediately repeat it one more time. After that, work that same exercise at the end of the session or in a future training session. Exercises that the dog knows very well can be worked out only once or, when the dog really likes them, twice per training session.

The proverb "You'll catch more flies with a spoonful of honey than with a barrel full of vinegar" applies in dog training. With gentleness we can achieve much more than with a harsh or brutal attitude. Dogs are extremely sensitive animals that react better to rewards than to punishment. In dog training, the right reward is the "magical" device. The dog likes to work out some exercises more than others, and that's why, after completing an unpleasant exercise, you should do an exercise the dog likes. And after five to 10 minutes of intensive training, take a break of about 15 minutes, in which the dog is totally free to relax.

Dogs like to work out some exercises more than others.

If you find you are not succeeding at a certain exercise, and you recognize that you're getting frustrated or angry, break off work on that exercise, because otherwise it will "go wrong." Take a walk for a while with your dog, or play with her with her ball, and try to think about something else for 10 minutes. Then start again with an exercise your dog likes to do, because that motivates both of you. If your dog is having an off day, try to think of what might be causing it. Don't always blame the dog; perhaps you are the one having the off day.

5

Basic Education and Exercises

When talking about giving their dogs an "education," people generally mean teaching the dog to Heel on Leash, Sit, Down, and to break certain bad habits. An education teaches the dog some basic manners. However, we have another view on educating dogs. Before anything happens in a young dog's training, she must be prepared for her future tasks and learn how to behave well. If you start to exercise your young dog in the direction of her skills—i.e., she is being educated to work—she will definitely learn to behave herself. Consider humans: it is correctly said that childhood, or education, leaves a mark on the child's whole life. The same can be true about dogs. The education of a future protection dog has to be directed toward two important parts: obedience and protection training.

In training, we must follow the right approach. Obedience is the keystone to all training because a protection dog must always be under the control of her handler and must always directly obey her handler's commands, such as the commands to stay or to come. For her there should be nothing more important than the word of her handler. A disobedient dog can never be a good protection dog.

In obedience exercises, we distinguish between direct and indirect obedience. The Recall, Heel, and Wait exercises, and

Before anything happens in a young dog's training, she must be prepared for her future tasks.

not performing certain bad habits, are examples of direct obedience. Performing exercises the dog has been taught, like barking, jumping, retrieving, and tracking, are forms of indirect obedience, which arise from direct obedience.

Recall

From her earliest youth, the dog must be used to the direct form of obedience. Later on, she has to come quickly and without delay on command, or to a whistle, to her handler. Avoid high-pressure tactics in teaching obedience. Instead, use weak mental pressure to bring her around to obedient behavior.

When it's meal time and your dog's food is ready, call her with "Come" or "Here." Before giving her the food, walk with her for a few minutes or ask someone to hold her, and after you walk a few feet away from her with the food bowl, call her to you and then give her the food. This is a pleasant way to encourage your dog to come to you. When you do this without a food reward, reward your dog exuberantly when she comes. Eventually give her a dog biscuit or something like that as a reward. Later, add a whistle before speaking the command so she will become used to that. Then alternate by blowing the whistle and using your voice to call her.

Getting Used to the Leash

When your dog is about two months old, let her gain some experience of the outside world. Moving around in fresh air will not only give her new experiences but also necessary physical development.

When she is on the street with you, your young dog should be on leash for the first while. Later on, when she is older and heels correctly, you can start teaching her to heel off leash on streets where there is little or no traffic. If you make your dog heel on leash all the time, she can become clingy and will always stay close to you. This may be nice for you in some ways—you don't have to watch your dog every minute—but too much on-leash heeling gives the dog too little freedom of movement and makes her too dependent.

In the beginning, use a simple leather collar with a ring for the leash. The collar has to be tight enough so that it cannot slip over the head of the dog, but not so tight that it chokes her. With your dog on leash, quietly walk a few steps without paying too much attention to the resistance your puppy will put up at the unusual pressure. After a few paces, stand still, pet her and talk to her in a friendly way.

At this point it doesn't matter what side the dog is walking on; the primarily goal at first is to make sure that she doesn't experience the walk on leash as a disaster. Normally, after a while, the young dog gets quieter on the walks. Once she is walking on leash better, and you are far away from traffic, you can let her walk free.

But before you take away the leash, entice her while walking quietly backward, saying "Here" (or "Come"), "Good girl, here!" If she obeys, you can, in a safe place, let her off leash and call, "Free."

Gradually, as your dog gets older, she will become used to walking correctly on your left side because you will always ensure she is on your left. If she pulls forward or sideways while she is walking with you on leash, you can use a reward to help her learn not to do that. We have to keep in mind that dogs will not learn everything overnight. By talking to your dog, you hold her attention. So, when your dog is pulling the wrong way while you walk, quietly talk to her: "Hey girl, don't walk faster than I do." You then coax her back by showing her a piece of food that you are holding in your left hand and speak the command, "Heel." If she walks correctly for a few steps after that, praise her, "Good girl," and give her another reward.

Never resort to violence, or pressure your young dog, but instead use rewards, such as food (in the example above), balls on ropes, several types of tugs, and so on. Choose the reward—or rewards, if you want to mix it up—that best fits your dog, making sure that she likes the rewards she is given. It doesn't matter if you like the

Movement is as important to your dog's physical health as a good diet.

reward: the dog has to like it. To introduce a new toy, for example, which will serve as a reward, play with your dog and the ball or tug by moving it quickly and throwing it, and so on. Soon, your dog will like the toy very much, and you can introduce it to training.

Stay and Lie Down

Your dog has to learn to stay at a spot indicated by you until you come back. Most of the time, this exercise is trained by teaching the dog to stay in the Down position. This, however, connects two training parts, "Down" and "Stay," making the training more difficult. In reality, it is impractical for the protection dog to always lie down when she has to stay somewhere for a long time. A protection dog may need to stay in a variety of circumstances: cold and wet weather, in front of a house on a busy street, and so on. The dog may be forced to sit or stand because of the weather or people touching or stepping over her, or by other circumstances. If this happens, her understanding that she must "stay in place" may be lost, because she may only connect Stay with Down. Once she's up, she may leave her spot.

Using our method, you teach your dog the Down and Stay as separate exercises. The essence of Stay is that the dog stays where you want her to, for as long as you want her to. We believe it is unimportant how she does it: sitting, lying, or standing. By teaching a dog to wait in a position of her own choice, dog and handler are spared a lot of unpleasant moments. Using our method, you will teach her to stay in place without force, and so you can train this exercise with even a young dog.

The best approach is to train somewhere outside, in a courtyard, in the garden, in the wood, or in a meadow. There should be something handy to which you can tie your dog, like a tree, shrub, or fence. Once you fasten the leash, slowly walk away and say the command "Wait" or "Stay." In the first session, don't go too far away from your dog, and stay in her sight. Walk around a bit and keep saying "Wait" or "Stay."

If your dog isn't quiet, don't react to that, or else she learns to get attention this way. Of course, we have to ensure that our dogs are not strangling on the leash or chewing on it, so while you are walking around, observe your dog from time to time. If your dog starts to bite her leash, stop the exercise immediately, and next time use a light chain instead of a leash.

If everything is going well and your dog stays quiet, go back to her after a few minutes and praise her, "Good girl, wait [or stay]," pet her, and again walk away while saying the command "Wait" (or "Stay"). When you finally come back to her, praise her again. At this point, let her free to play, and after some time repeat the exercise.

After some training of Stay, you gradually advance farther away from your dog, stay away for a longer time, and leave the dog's sight. In this way, you train the dog to stay in every possible situation, even in the house. As well, whenever you take your dog somewhere and need to leave her outside a shop, for example, tether her and give her the command to "Stay" or "Wait." This combination of exercises helps your dog learn the Stay faster and remember it better than being taught the Stay exercise only at certain places.

Using Waiting Time Well

Now, a word about the handler who finds he must wait; a lot of time at a training field is spent waiting. Let us assure you that any "lost" time, even spent waiting, is your own fault, because in fact there is much you can do while waiting. When doing protection dog training in a group, there are always moments when we have to wait for our colleagues. Using that time to look at the training of these other handlers and their dogs can be profitable. We can learn much from the mistakes and problems of other handlers. By watching what is going wrong and hearing the discussion of possible solutions, we can gain the advantage. We are never too old or too experienced to learn, especially about dogs.

When you have to wait at the training field, your dog does, too. She is not bored, but is paying attention to all kinds of things happening around her on the field. We often see handlers talking to their neighbors instead of paying attention to their dog. When the group training continues, these handlers most of the time hastily break off their conversation with the other handlers and take their places in the row. But did they check their dog before trying to work out the instructor's commands? And do they know what they are supposed to do? After all, they weren't paying attention, and neither were their dogs.

Such inattentiveness can mean a failure of the exercise, because for dog training, two attentive individuals are needed. Think about it: you can't train a dog with just commands and a leash. You need

The education of a future protection dog has two important parts: obedience and protection training.

contact. In dog training, the contact between handler and dog is the most important thing. So instead of chatting while you wait, work on having better contact with your dog. Even waiting has to be taught.

Jumping

Movement is as important to the health of a young dog as good food is. But before your dog is six months old, you must not allow her to make high jumps. Until that age, you should take your dog out into the fresh air as much as possible, where she already has the opportunity to make little jumps over low-lying shrubs, fallen trees, and other things that are low to the ground and will not harm her ongoing development. (Note that the jumping movements a young dog makes all by herself are part of normal development and under normal circumstances are not forbidden.) Remember that when you do begin to teach your dog to jump, she must first be reasonably obedient and able to heel on leash.

After six months, you can slowly prepare your dog for jumping. Teaching her how to jump at a young age saves a lot of training later on. Besides, specific training at that age can contribute to bone and muscle strength; by this we assume the dog is already in good health, with correctly developed bones.

When you begin jumping exercises, it's important to pay attention to the sort of obstacle you use and its height. Use a closed obstacle, where the dog has no opportunity to go under. Furthermore, in the beginning, the obstacle should only be chest-high on the dog. Then, when everything is going well, and you have trained for at least one month, the obstacle can slowly be made higher. If that is also successful, then one month later the obstacle can again be made higher.

Until the age of nine months, you should not allow medium-sized and large dogs to jump higher than 20 inches (50 cm). The dog should not jump anything higher than 28 inches (70 cm) until she is at least one year or, better, 18 months old. The body of the young dog is still in development and can, with moderate jumping, be made stronger. Overexertion, however, causes damage, and that's why we teach the young dog the command for jumping with low obstacles. When she knows the command and how to jump, she won't have trouble with higher obstacles when she is older.

For the first jumping exercises, put your dog on leash and walk quietly to the low obstacle. About seven feet (2 m) before it, say, "Attention," followed by "Hup" (or "Jump" or "High"). Picking up speed, advance toward the obstacle and jump over it—your dog should follow you. As soon as the young dog jumps, say, "Hup, good girl, hup," and after that, praise her with exuberance. After giving lots of praise, turn around and repeat the exercise, jumping back over the obstacle.

A bull terrier jumps high in front of the decoy during the Hold and Bark exercise.

If your dog doesn't want to jump with you, try making the obstacle lower. Never pull your dog over the obstacle. When she starts jumping over the obstacle by herself, ensure she takes a running start to jump back over it. To do this, you have to run alongside the obstacle to the other side and then entice your dog to move at least seven feet away from the obstacle before allowing her to run and jump back over it.

Remember never to press your dog to jump too many times in a row. Three times there and back is more than enough. These jumping exercises eventually can be repeated two to three times an hour. But be mindful of the biggest danger in dog training: overdoing it.

6

Stopping Bad Behavior

While exploring their environment, young dogs also like to play all sorts of naughty tricks. Most of these don't develop into big problems, but some do and become the start of really bad behavior. The practical value of the dog can be diminished by bad habits. But we have to understand that the actions we chalk up to bad behavior are actually lots of fun for the dog. Otherwise she would not do them.

We distinguish between two sorts of bad habits: the innate and those acquired by education. Innate bad behavior characteristics originate from the unique disposition of the forebears of our dogs. Most of these behaviors are related to food acquisition, like the unwanted hunting of game, birds, and so on; stealing food from the table or kitchen; or running after and barking at cyclists and vehicles. Eating droppings and wallowing in them can also be counted as bad habits, as well as biting to pieces and chewing on all sorts of articles. Bad habits acquired through education include leaping up on people, not being house-trained, and opening doors.

Unwanted Hunting

We normally will not see the proclivity to hunt game in the young dog. But we do see the beginnings of it when puppies chase birds. Although the chances are not great that the still-awkward dog will ever catch a bird, from the beginning we must make it clear to her that we cannot allow such games.

In stopping bad habits, more than anything else it is necessary that the dog be caught in the act and immediately punished. Therefore, we say, "No," in a sharp, reprimanding tone, which for most young dogs will be enough. Immediately correcting the young dog from the beginning saves you a lot of annoyance—and the dog a lot of punishment—later. If you notice that your young dog already has an interest in birds, take her on leash and bring her, with a slack leash, as close as possible to a place with, for instance, chickens. If she makes even a small move to run after a chicken, then she should immediately be punished by a sharply spoken "No!" After that, walk with her closer to the chickens (or other birds) and try, when that is going well, to walk among them. Every attempt to run after the birds should be punished. If your dog is doing well, then praise her, of course. It is also possible to distract her from focusing on the chickens by having some food in your hand. In fact, most of the time, the food reward/distraction is even more effective for young dogs than spoken punishment. Every now and then, give her some food to reward her for her good behavior.

We'd like to remind you that with a young dog punishment has to be well-balanced. In general, if you follow our suggestions, don't think that the punishment you are giving is too harsh. If the punishment temporarily weakens the confidence between you and your dog, this is less serious than a too-weak punishment. The latter doesn't impress the dog, so later on she will make the same mistakes again and will have to be punished constantly.

PUNISHMENT

For a young dog, birds are very enticing; full of enthusiasm, she will run after them. Although it is nice to see the dog running over the fields, and as good as this movement may be for her physical development, it damages her obedience and ability to devote herself later to her tasks as a protection dog. This innocent running after birds switches to running after game, and even after livestock, with unpleasant results for the livestock and also for the dog's obedience skills.

By now, your dog knows the word "No" is a punishment, and that's why it has to be used with every punishment, so she will no longer run after birds or other animals. If she doesn't react to "No," giving her a punishment when she returns to you is incorrect. She then will connect the punishment with coming to you, her handler, and because of that she will shy away from returning next time and be even more confused if you punish her again. If she returns to you, it is better to forget punishment for the moment. It is better to take her on leash and try to approach the birds and distract her with food in hand. If she is still interested in chasing the birds, immediately punish her with a sharply spoken "No!"

You can punish an unleashed dog by throwing a chain collar or a tin filled with stones. If you punish your dog this way, don't call her first. If the throw was successful, that is, the dog was startled by the chain or can falling beside her (never on her), yell, "No!" Then, call her back to you and put her on leash; only after that do you pick up the thrown chain or can.

Stealing Food

An uneducated dog will see everything edible and reachable as loot, without being aware that she should not simply take what she wants. It has to be made clear that this kind of behavior is undesirable, and it is not necessary to wait for the first violation. It's hard to catch dogs in the act of stealing food, and punishing them after the fact doesn't make sense because they will not know what they are being punished for. Because of that, it's better to lead the dog into temptation, so to speak, so that she can be punished immediately.

Sometimes protection
work looks like dancing.

Bring your dog into the kitchen, where you have already laid some pieces of meat on a plate in a place she can reach, perhaps on a low shelf, the cupboard door partly open. Give your dog a chance to catch the scent of the meat. Stand nonchalantly and say nothing to your dog, or even wait out of sight to observe her actions.

If she goes to that cupboard, wait very quietly. Only when she tries to open the cupboard door should you interfere with "No!" We have to be patient, because sometimes it takes time before the dog is enticed by the food. Some dogs need to be tempted and punished several times before they get the message, perhaps because the initial punishment was too gentle.

Eating Droppings

Young dogs have a great liking for eating the droppings of people, horses, cows, and other animals. But adult dogs also like it, and just as young dogs do, they sometimes wallow in all sorts of stinking carrion. You must always watch your off-leash dog closely and observe what she is doing. If she suddenly leaves her pursuits and walks straight to a spot, it may be because there is an odor there of food, carrion, or droppings.

Try to approach your dog as nonchalantly as possible and have a look at what caught her interest. If necessary, startle her with a sharp "No!" If it's clear that your dog has already eaten the carrion or droppings, take her away, put her on leash, and then walk back to where the carrion is. Let her walk in front so that she catches the odor and possibly shows interest again. Then, again, clearly say, "No!" After that, keep your dog on leash for some time during walks outside.

Wallowing in Mud

If you see your dog rolling in mud or offal, throw a clump of grass, a piece of wood, or a handful of pebbles in her direction to startle her. Don't use the chain collar or the tin with pebbles this time, as you don't want to have to pick it up out of the mud. If you startle your dog, immediately yell, "No!"

Remember this location well. Your dog, of course, will need a bath when you get home. Several hours later, or the next day, walk to that place again, but this time with her on leash. If she shows interest in the mud or offal, punish her again, and again put her on leash for a while during walks.

Other times, protection work looks like acrobatics.

House-training

Some things that seem innocent in the beginning will, if we pay no attention to them, soon become undesirable habits, such as a lack of house-training. To house-train a young dog, the following general rules apply. When the young one wakes up after a sleep, she always should be brought out immediately. She should also be taken outside after she has drunk a lot of water, after intensive playing, after each meal, and even if she is simply walking restlessly through the house. If you let the dog out even more often, she will very quickly get used to relieving herself only outside.

Say the same words every time your dog has to go because she'll get used to voiding as soon as she hears those words. We can say, for instance, "Go pee/poop," or "Lift your leg." By teaching the dog a command associated with the action, you can help her manage her needs, depending on the circumstances, which will be invaluable later.

It makes no sense to punish a young dog for not being house-trained; and it's even worse to punish a dog by pushing her nose into her droppings. The younger the dog, the faster her digestion is, so, she will have to go several times a day. If a dog is older than, say, four months, an "accident" can provoke a mild punishment. That means that only when we see it happening will we grumble at her and carry her outside quickly. Outside she is, whether she does something or not, every time a "Good girl."

The decoy is forced to surrender.

If your puppy piddles near the outside door, she was trying to go in the right direction. If the door had been open, she would have gone outside. She just doesn't know how to make it clear to you that she has to go outside, or you did not understand her. To understand her "language," remember to observe her closely. Not all dogs make it clear to us that they have to go by scratching the door or barking. A lot of dogs walk to a member of the family and only look at him or her; some lay their paw or head on a family member's knee, while others walk restlessly through the room and whine softly. If a dog shows in one way or the other that she has to go, praise her and take her outside. And don't forget to praise her there, as well, for her correct behavior.

If the dog is not clear in her signals that she has to go, you can teach her to be clear by bringing her outside at fixed times. Put her on leash and bring her to the outside door whenever you say, "Go pee/poop" or "Lift your leg." If she goes outside, praise her for her good behavior. Note that if your dog has already learned to bark on command, stay in front of the door and let her bark a few times before you go outside.

Running after Moving Objects

Another undesirable behavior is barking at or running after cyclists, motorcycles, cars, and other moving vehicles. Normally, pups and young dogs don't have this bad and dangerous habit. The behavior usually develops during the dog's puberty, so from about six months until the age of over one year, usually when the dog has the opportunity to be outside without supervision, as in a yard bordering a road.

A dog that is supervised by her owners will not so easily develop this bad habit, because when she shows the inclination, it is immediately forbidden by "No!" But dogs between seven and 14 months sometimes act very tough. She may like to bark and run after cyclists and cars because all fast-moving things prickle her hunting drive. This is not only the case for hunting dogs—all dogs have a hunting drive. Most dogs are not hostile to the cyclist: when the latter stands still or gets off, the animal soon loses interest.

To break a dog of the habit of running after moving objects, divert her. You can accomplish this with the help of a well-known person who you engage to cycle by your house. While the person is riding by, distract your dog with food in your hand. If normal dog food isn't enough of an enticement, try something that is more of a treat, such as a piece of cheese.

If an older dog runs after cyclists or cars, and she doesn't react to the food-in-your-hand trick, you have to catch her in the act and punish her. The punishment could be the tin with pebbles thrown in her direction and a sharp "No!" If she doesn't even react to this, probably because of a bad education during her youth, take stronger measures because this habit is really dangerous and can take her life. The next step is to use a choke-chain collar. Ensure the collar is put around her neck in the right way: that means the part coming over the top of the neck has to come through the ring coming from the underside. Fasten her leash on the free ring. The part with the free ring, on which the leash is fastened, always has to come from the upside of the dog's neck. See pages 92 and 93 for complete directions on the use of this collar. To the leash you fasten a correctly rolled line, about 33 feet (10 m) long, and you keep the end of the line firmly in hand.

If a car approaches, watch to see if your dog shows interest, but say nothing. Keep such a distance from the road that your dog cannot get hit. If she runs after the car, let the long line unwind till she comes to the end and the choke chain pulls tightly. At the same time, punish her with "No!" The more powerful the jerk is, the better this will work. This is why it's so important for the chain collar to be put on correctly: as soon as the dog stops pulling, the chain collar opens all by itself, and the dog is unharmed—only frightened.

It is very important that this long-line punishment is effective; you cannot repeat this punishment in this way again, or your dog may learn that she must not run after moving objects only when she is on the long line. The dangerous habit of running after cars will not be stopped. Again fasten the long line to the normal leash on the collar. This time, hold the leash, keeping it stretched taut at first, but soon let it go slack. If the dog now shows interest in a car or cyclist, drop the short leash. Your dog may think, in her excitement, that she is free but she will run up against that long line again.

To prevent a dog from falling back into old mistakes, you also can call her to heel when a car or cyclist is heard or appears, immediately give her a food reward for listening, and then take her on leash. In time, some dogs who undergo this series of punishments and rewards will come to their handlers and heel themselves when they hear an engine or see a car or cyclist. Of course, directly reward this good behavior with a dog biscuit or other treat.

Leaping Up

Many dogs show their love and joy by leaping up on us. Even if your dog is showing her devotion to you, that is not always pleasant, especially when she wants to leap up onto your nice suit with her muddy paws. However, a young dog must not be warded off too harshly, because her confidence in her handler can take a terrible knock. A strong bond between you and your dog is crucial, and touching plays an important role in that bond.

Instead, your young dog has to understand when she can jump up on you and when she cannot. If you don't want her to jump, keep her away in a friendly but clear manner. Try to catch her in the jump, before she touches you with her front legs; then, give her a light push to the left with your right hand and step quickly to your right. As you do that, give the command "Don't jump." After a short time, your dog will understand this "not jumping," and the meaning of a hand held up as a deterrent.

A dog with the right courage and fighting instincts.

In older dogs that are not well-educated, you can also bring up a knee as a deterrent, which will hinder her jumping. There are also dogs that, in their enthusiasm, jump up from the ground with all four legs. With such dogs, you have to take more evasive maneuvers to avoid them, but you can normally correct such enthusiastic dogs with your voice. And if you don't want a dog to jump up at all, you have to use the deterrent movement with a harshly spoken "No!"

Opening Doors

Dogs become very troublesome when they open doors all by themselves. Such dogs are ill-mannered, not stupid. A dog must, however, learn to stay in place on command; she is not allowed to walk all through the house without our permission. That's why she has to have her own place in the house. If your young dog tries to open doors, you have to catch her in the act, but she probably won't engage in this behavior unless she thinks you are out of the house. That's why we recommend that you use a baby monitor to catch her out, or you can try to observe her behavior through a window from outside.

It may take a while before the jumping up against doors and the opening of doors starts. Normally, the dog feels lonely first and walks around whining, and then she tries to open the door. When she jumps up to the door, she immediately must be punished with a harsh and powerful "No!" Remember that your dog's feeling of loneliness can often be assuaged if you leave the radio or TV on when you are out of the house.

Finally, a brief word about dogs kept in kennels and that only come into the house now and then. Kennel dogs must first have time to run and stretch outside to let off steam before they will feel "at home" in the house. But in spite of that, a lot of kennel dogs will never feel at home in the house, simply because they don't have enough contact with people.

Obedience

7

Training for Heelwork

If you plan to train your dog to become a protection dog, it is never too early to start training him to do the different exercises. The breeder can stimulate heelwork in four-week-old pups. While walking, you can entice your off-leash pup to walk with you by showing him how, and now and then giving him a treat. If the pup is about seven weeks old, you can also walk with him on leash. When you do this every day for just a few minutes in your yard or living room, your pup gets used to walking beside you, and he will never walk behind you. Pups that have been "trained" this way can do amazing heelwork at a very young age because they have learned to focus their attention on their handlers. Pups, of course, are older than four weeks when they come to their new owners. But you can do the same with an eight-week-old pup: have him walk beside you and pay attention to you.

Equipment

For obedience training, we advise you to use a chain collar, a so-called choke chain. If you're training a sensitive dog (or a pup) that doesn't regularly need serious corrections (or that is frightened), you can also use a leather or nylon collar. To that chain or collar has to be fastened a long, pliable leather leash. Every other type of line can damage your hands if you have to correct your dog.

For the chain collar to work correctly, how you place it around your dog's neck is crucial. The chain should not slip around the neck as the noose is closing, because that can damage your dog's coat or hurt him. Take one of the rings at the end of the chain and slip the other end through this ring, creating a closed collar. Ask your dog to sit at your left side. Slip the chain over his head so that the free ring comes down from the top side of his neck to the right side. When you affix the leash now, the free ring that pulls the chain is going to close very quickly, without slipping around his neck and cutting his hair off. When you slip the chain on the wrong way, so that the ring fixed on the leash comes from under the neck, then the whole chain slides around the neck as it tightens and damages hair and even skin. As well, when put on improperly, the chain collar won't open by itself after it has pulled tight. Furthermore, the chain has to be the right length, which means it should go over your dog's head with, just like a normal collar, only a little room to spare.

If it fits correctly around the neck, there should be at most two inches (5 cm) of the chain pulling through before the chain is snug. There are chains with a so-called key ring at one end to make the chain the right size. Long chains take too long to have an effect when used; too tight a chain will cause your dog discomfort when you pull it over his head, and when it is too tight around the neck, it gives him a constant "choking" feeling.

A chain collar can also be arranged not to choke if you affix the leash to both rings. Then the noosing effect is lost, and your dog can pull his head out of the chain. A 33-foot-(10-m-) long line is also standard equipment for further training.

Be careful when putting a chain collar on your dog; if you put it on incorrectly, it can cause your dog discomfort or simply not be effective. This photo shows the correct way.

Correct heelwork is also important when you start training your dog to be a protection dog, such as in the Back Transport exercise.

The Best Time to Train

As you embark on training, remember there are better times than others during the day to train a puppy. In general, the best time is when your dog is neither too tired nor too active (of course that depends on the age, personality, and breed of the dog). Five or 10 minutes before he gets his food is an ideal time to train, especially when he knows that it's time to eat. When his food bowl stands ready on the kitchen counter, he will very soon understand that training is going to be rewarded, and that he has to work for his food.

A dog in this situation has no problem with training and is inclined to pay more attention to you. In the beginning, two five-minute training sessions are much better than 10 minutes in a row. Always end the training time with a successful exercise; even if it's just a simple one.

Not Pulling

A lot of people think that heelwork is just "not pulling on the leash," which causes a lot of entanglement. When you're on a normal outing, your dog doesn't necessarily have to heel, but he isn't allowed to pull on the leash, either. Doing heelwork all the time is much too strenuous and tiring for handler and dog.

"Not pulling on the leash" is the normal way to walk on leash. If your young dog pulls, he has to be corrected with a short, but powerful, "No!" or "Don't pull," or you can show him some food in your hand that you give him when he is walking correctly, without pulling on the leash. When he knows that food is there, he will stay close to you and give you his attention. The command "Heel" must not be used at this point. "Not pulling" can be taught and perfected if you walk with your dog around posts and trees, making sure your dog is attentive at all times.

Training Heelwork

Heelwork is a real obedience exercise that has to be worked out as perfectly as possible. It is the same sort of exercise as Sit and Down. In all sorts of training, the dog normally walks on his handler's left side, which is a holdover from police dog training. Dogs in police service were trained to walk on the left of their handlers because a police officer walking down a street would be protected on the right by houses or fences, but danger could approach from the left. As well, most people are right-handed, so the police officer, holding the dog on the left, would have the right hand free to hold a weapon. In Chapter 15, "The Dutch Police Dog Test," you will read that police dogs, while heeling off leash, must be able to switch on command from the handler's right side to the left, and from the left side to the right.

The starting point in heeling is for your dog to sit correctly at your left side with his nose pointed in the direction you want to walk. The leash should hang slack in a U-shape between you and your dog. Hold the leash with your right hand.

Say your dog's name, but stand still. This is so your dog begins the exercise by paying attention to you, his handler. Than say, "Heel," wait a beat, and take a clear step forward. When you start to walk, your dog should also begin walking, especially if it looks like something interesting is going to happen.

If all is going well, your dog should be walking correctly and attentive, with a U-bend in the leash at a four-inch (10-cm) distance from you, with his head in line with your knee. Remember that in the beginning, though, most dogs will either walk in front, behind, or much too far away from their handlers. This behavior must, of course, be avoided. The easiest way to stop your dog from walking incorrectly is to hold some dog biscuits or cheese in your left hand, and as you walk, every now and then give him some treats. As he gets better at heeling, make the time between treats longer and longer.

Things work well with pups when we also talk to them in a pleasant tonc and keep them attentive. In the beginning, heelwork with pups should only last a few minutes at a time—again, always finish with a positive experience.

Kicking up his heels.

Little Helpers

The most important thing in heelwork is for your dog to be attentive to you. If he is doing well in this regard, that U-shaped leash should hang between the two of you. You can get and hold your dog's attention by making the training exciting and fun. In teaching an exercise, you can make use of things the dog likes. A ball in the right hand holds some dogs' attention very well because there is the promise of playing with the ball at the end of the session. For other dogs, a retrieving article is best; again, keep it in your right hand, and after the exercise let him retrieve. Dogs with big appetites can be made attentive by a piece of cheese or sausage. However, the danger of introducing these little helpers is that your dog may get excited and walk ahead of you or jump up on you; immediately let him know that's not what you want.

Dogs that lag behind can be enticed to speed up when you run a little. This should not encourage him to jump while he runs; the point here is for him to trot quietly beside you. Walk in an energetic tempo; the more energetic it is, the less the dog is tempted to wander, pull, or sniff. However, the most important encouragement to dogs learning to heel is their handlers' enthusiasm. A handler who moves actively and shows energy passes that on to his or her dog. We always see a lethargic dog with a lethargic handler.

The Hold and Bark, another way.

Turns

The first times you train for heelwork, you'll find that the turn to the left is the simplest to work out. Walk straight on and then make a 90° turn to the left (a right-angle turn). If your dog wasn't attentive when you turned, he will be surprised. If you walk against his head when you make the turn, he will learn to stay more attentive. Take care that his head is indeed in line with your knee when you take the turn, otherwise the turn will be odd, and your dog may begin to feel insecure about turns.

The turn to the right is more difficult because the dog walks on the outside of the turn, and you can't make him attentive with your body. But do not jerk automatically on the leash when you turn to the right. First, try to get your dog's attention with your voice and food in your hand. Later on make 45° turns to the left and right.

Dogs that pull on the leash must first do the turn to the left very well and show that they are attentive before you can show them the turn to the right. Don't stand still with the turns, but train yourselves to round the corner in a flowing movement. Dogs that like a ball, a retrieving article, or a snack can be tempted to make perfect right-angle turns by using those little helpers.

The About-turn

The left about-turn is also a lot easier to train than the right turn is. With this turn, start with the left about-turn, and make a 180° turn to face the direction from which you came. It works as follows: walk in a straight line and turn with your dog on the inside back toward the direction you came from. To complete the exercise, your dog has to remain attentive because he has to turn very fast, or he will be knocked over.

Most dogs understand how to do the about-turn quickly, and the exercise seldom gives problems. Even the most persistently leash-pulling dog can learn to work this exercise out correctly, and learning it will help him be more attentive to heelwork in general. Handlers often have the inclination to walk in little bends, but the

Always finish up a training session with an exercise that your dog does well.

left about-turn has to be done in the space of two, or at most three (with a big dog), paces, flowing and without standing still.

The right about-turn is more difficult, and in the beginning your dog must be made extra attentive to get it right. Call his name when you begin. Remember that for the right about-turn, your dog will be walking on the outside, so make sure you entice him into walking correctly with you.

Make sure you don't stand still when you start either the left or right about-turn. If you tend to stand still before starting the turn, train without a dog until you can execute the turn in one flowing motion by yourself. If you stand still or decrease your tempo before the turn, your dog will learn to do the same, which causes problems with the about-turn later in training.

How Long Should You Train?

Training twice a day for five minutes is more than enough to start. In the beginning, only train correct heeling straight on, and then add the turn to the left. Later on, add the turn to the right, and the left about-turn. When this is working out correctly, bring the right about-turn into the mix. Use the leash as little as possible, because

Impressive and spectacular bite work.

later on all exercises have to be performed off leash. What you accomplish with your voice and those little helpers we mention above will also help your dog learn off-leash heeling.

The five-minute exercises can, of course, be divided into one-minute sessions, for which your dog is rewarded by playing. When playing, keep your dog on leash and keep him focused on you. Teach your dog that with the word "Enough," he has to be quiet again and the training continues. During such breaks, don't allow your dog to play with other dogs, because his attention has to be focused on you. Always be kind to your dog, not only because that will encourage him to work for you with pleasure, but also to build a strong handler-dog bond. Always finish training with an exercise that has a positive result, such as a small piece of straight heelwork followed by some reward play. Make sure his food bowl is waiting for him at home, which will double his pleasure in training.

8

Training the Sit

Normal "sitting" differs greatly from the correct Sit at Heel or the correct Sit after Come-fore (the correct Sit in this case is facing you, not on your left side). It's difficult to train your dog to stay sitting when something exciting happens in front of him, such as when you are on the field during protection training. Generally, the first exercise people teach their pups is the Sit. It is a reasonably easy exercise, because a normal dog, given the right reward (dog-biscuit, cheese, sausage, or dog food), very quickly understands what is going on. Besides, it is only teaching a command word. The dog regularly sits all by himself. Now he only has to learn to do that when his handler says, "Sit" to him.

The Sit as a basic exercise normally gives few problems, but it becomes more difficult when it is coupled with other exercises. Then the dog is expected to sit without an explicit command or to stay in the Sit position. In almost all forms of dog training, exercises start from the Sit position. The dog is then sitting at the left side of his handler, hopefully attentive in anticipation that something will happen. The correct way of sitting is straight and close beside the handler, with dog's nose pointed toward the direction of the action.

A Useful Exercise

Sitting is a particularly useful exercise for situations in daily life, regardless of whether or not your dog trains for protection work. A sitting dog will be less inclined to move than a standing dog. When taking a break during a walk, it is good to let the dog sit. When you, for example, stop for a chat with someone with or without a dog, if your dog sits, you will not be interrupted by sniffing, pulling, or jumping up. At curbs, the well-educated dog automatically sits down, at least if his handler also stops, and he doesn't cross the street without thinking. At a traffic light, handler and dog have to stop and wait quietly until they can cross the street; the dog has to wait in the Sit position.

The Sit performed in a special way during police surveillance.

This dog has truly mastered the Sit. Nowadays, dogs are only allowed to bite the legs of a cycling helper.

We know a woman who had a very strong male dog, a German shepherd that was never taught to sit at curbs. One time the dog pulled her into busy traffic, and her arm was broken. When you teach your young dog to sit down immediately at a stop, such accidents cannot happen, no matter how strong your dog is.

Pressing Down

There are different ways to teach a dog to sit. The most used one is the mechanical way, by saying "Sit" as you push down on the dog's back end. In general, this will work with pups and small or lightly built dogs. But it is not a very responsible way of teaching the Sit because with more heavily built pups or dogs, it is possible that the pressure on the back end can contribute to damaging the vertebral joints and hips.

Teaching the Sit by pushing can also cause other problems. Some dogs like being pushed on the back end and they counter it by pushing back up. For these dogs, the mechanical method will definitely not lead very quickly to the desired Sit. Such an enthusiastic "counter pusher" shouldn't be touched at all while learning the Sit, or the Down, for that matter. They learn these exercises better through signals and rewards.

The Natural Way

Every dog is inclined to sit when he has to look up high. We can make use of this inclination in teaching the Sit exercise. The method used most to correctly teach the Sit is to pull the leash upward with one hand (the dog then looks up) and at the same time touch the back end of the dog. Use your middle finger in the space between the last rib and the beginning of the back leg, while your thumb and the forefinger rest on your dog's back. With this method, there is no pressure on your dog's hips. This pulling and touching must happen at the same time, calmly and with care, so your dog doesn't experience it as unpleasant. As you bring your dog to sit, use a clear command: "Sit." When he is sitting, praise and pet him, and eventually give him

For the dog, it often doesn't seem logical to wait any longer before taking action.

a treat. Note that some dogs will sit by themselves if their handlers get them to look up high by holding up a reward in their hand.

Sitting in Front

The "look up high method" also works well with the Recall and Sit in Front exercises, where success depends largely on the dog correctly sitting in front of the handler. For this exercise, the dog sits off leash, or is kept on leash by a helper, with his head and attention pointed at his handler. The handler takes a treat or a ball out of his or her pocket and keeps it at the dog's eye level with two hands in front. Then the dog is called—most of the time he runs straight to his handler. Then the handler takes a step backward and moves his or her hands straight up (with a medium-sized dog, to the level of the handler's chest). An attentive, properly trained dog will then correctly sit in front of his handler, even if the command "Sit" is not spoken. Of course, the command must be given and, after a brief pause to keep his attention, the handler gives the dog his reward. The reward must be offered with both hands; otherwise, the dog will sit facing the hand with the reward and won't be sitting correctly in front of the handler anymore. Younger dogs can be taught the Sit this way, without a "recall."

When he sits correctly, your dog should be rewarded. The form of the reward depends on you and your dog. For a long time, we used biscuits, broken into as many pieces as possible. By the time one cookie was consumed, our pup would know the Sit. Some dogs prefer to be petted as a reward. If your dog is like this, pet him when he is sitting and make sure he stays sitting as you pet him—pet him under his chin and not over his head. By stroking him under the chin, your dog will look up, which keeps him in position. If you choose to give a treat instead, offer it to him from above, for the same reason.

Canceling the Sit

As in all exercises, it should be you and not the dog who cancels the "Sit" command. Both handler and dog need to concentrate. The dog has to know the meaning of the command, and you have to remember to cancel the command.

In puppy training, a Sit exercise should only last a short time, making it possible for you to cancel the command. You can do that by saying "Free" or clapping your hands and letting your dog move freely. If your dog is working out the Sit exercise well, have him stay in that position until you say he can do something else, such as lie down ("Down"), walk with you ("Heel"), or play ("Free").

Increasing the time the dog is sitting has to happen gradually. Some trainers are so happy their dog is working out an exercise well that they expect too much of him and leave him too long in the Sit (or Down) position. The still not fully trained dog cannot keep his mind on what is required of him for so long, and mistakes result. Short training sessions, worked out correctly and cancelled only by the handler, are necessary ingredients for good obedience.

Sitting at the Side

Any time your dog is sitting beside you—because he must perform an exercise or he is at a stop during heelwork—he must perform the Sit correctly. If your dog is young or inexperienced, make sure you say "Sit" when he is standing beside you. If that doesn't work, show him the food you are carrying in your hand or the toy reward. If that doesn't work either, carefully pull your dog's head upward with the leash, while placing, as described before, your middle finger in the space between the last rib and the back leg. When your dog is finally sitting, reward him; but he must stay sitting.

The correct way of sitting is straight beside you, the handler. Your dog should not be leaning against your leg or sitting diagonally in front of you. The dog that is always leaning against the handler's leg can be stopped from doing so if you step aside when he is not expecting it.

Some dogs, often the smaller ones but also shepherds, always sit diagonally with respect to their handlers, so they can keep an eye on them. In general, these dogs are strongly focused on their handlers and are afraid to miss a cue. If your dog, after months of intensive training, still sits diagonally, spare yourself some trouble and just let him sit that way.

Society needs reliable protection dogs.

Stopping

When you stop during a walk or during heelwork, your dog has to sit correctly beside you without a command. This must only be trained when your dog knows what is meant by "Sit." As you walk, stop in a way that accentuates the stopping; for example, stand still with your feet close together (this will become a sign for your dog). As you stop, announce a clear "Sit." If he isn't immediately sitting, help him out in the gentle manner described previously. After some training at a stop, your dog will probably sit down all on his own. If he doesn't, try showing him his reward.

In the beginning, most dogs sit diagonally, too far ahead or too far to the side. You correct that by moving him with your hand into the correct position. Note that some dogs like to be manipulated this way and will wait for it. With such a dog, you might say, "Better," or move one or more steps ahead to give him the opportunity to get into the correct position. When he is sitting beside you, your dog may not walk before you command, "Heel." That means you can walk away from him (stepping forward with the right leg) while your dog stays in the Sit position.

Self-control

Sitting is the starting point of almost every exercise. A sitting dog can see as much of his environment as a standing one, but he is more likely to hold his place. A standing dog tends to take a step forward, as you will see in training for the Stand. In the protection exercises, your dog will have to sit, while in front of him all kinds of exciting things are happening. Staying in the Sit position and waiting for a command, seeing the decoy challenging him, demands a lot of self-control from a dog. It doesn't make sense to him that he should wait to take action, so it is your task to teach your dog to be obedient at such moments, to sit and wait. We want to have reliable protection dogs.

9

Training the Down

For dogs, the Down is the most comfortable position there is. It is the pose that uses the least amount of energy. The Down position is meant for waiting, rest, and sleep. Even energetic dogs pass a big part of the day lying down, although less than dogs of a heavy breed. We think that the energetic dogs are afraid they might miss something. Big, heavy dogs lie, if possible, almost the whole day and follow what's going on from that position. Smaller, active, and young dogs want to see everything, and they have much more energy for all forms of movement. Such dogs only lie down if they are resting or asleep, but even then they will spring to their feet at the least little thing.

Down on Command is easier for some dogs than for others. The heavy boys will see it as a welcome break, while the "actives" will have problems taking a compulsory "rest." Some smaller breeds, especially the short-legged ones, find Down on Command a really dull exercise. Normally, they try to make themselves as big as possible, because they hate it that they are smaller than other dogs. So, as easy as they sit and even stay for a longer time than bigger dogs in the Sit position, so tedious do they find lying down. If possible, these little dogs try to dodge the Down by sitting quickly again, or furtively not lying down by suspending themselves on their elbows.

These dogs need some extra attention when learning the Down, especially in waiting for the Down command to be cancelled.

Uncertain Dogs

We think there is a special category for young or somewhat uncertain dogs. Some bigger as well as smaller dogs don't like the Down because from that position they cannot immediately flee, if they think they have to. Going from lying to running is less easy than fleeing from Sit or Stand. Besides, when lying down, a dog is smaller, and uncertain dogs like to be "big" and to have a good view of their surroundings. Involuntary Down, especially in strange or threatening surroundings, is very difficult for dogs that are afraid. These are also the dogs that have problems with the Stay exercise. Nevertheless, it is important that these dogs learn to be obedient, even when they don't like it in the beginning. Later on, successfully performing the Down and Stay exercises will actually make their self-confidence stronger; success in these exercises will also increase their confidence in their handlers. Slowly, they realize that nothing nasty happens when they have to lie down.

These dogs also cause problems when their handlers leave them. Even two steps aside can make them crawl or in extreme cases even quiver. By teaching the Down in a consistent and quiet way, the uncertain dog will eventually see that the involuntary rest can also be a real rest.

Canceling

When you are teaching the Down, it is important to know how and when to cancel the exercise. You must have much insight, because in the beginning the command must be canceled rather quickly. It's a bit like quick-draw, because you must always cancel the command before your dog takes the initiative. When their dogs are doing the Down exercise well, a lot of handlers become careless. They allow their dogs to lie down for too long, which results in the dogs forgetting the command or canceling it on their own. It is up to you, the handler, to take care that the exercise will be canceled inside the time your dog can be expected to wait.

Canceling can happen by issuing another command, such as "Sit" or "Free." You can also clap your hands and say, "Free." Young dogs, no matter how obedient they are, cannot stay in position for five minutes. That's why we have to take care that an exercise always successfully ends with a pleasant "Free" and a reward.

Reliable Dogs

A dog that knows the Down exercise very well, which means he lies down until the command is canceled, is a pleasure to work with. If your dog has mastered the Down, you can take him with you to all sorts of events. You know you can "park" him in a corner or under the table at a coffee shop, out of sight. Also, you know that when you pause on a walk, your dog will not jump or pull, but will lie down. When after some time he lies down on his own, even when you are out of his sight, you know you can take him anywhere. That's the way it has to be for a protection dog.

Methods for Teaching the Down

The Down exercise can be taught to young puppies. The common method for doing this is the mechanical way: from the Sit position, the dog's front legs are pulled forward as the handler gives the command "Down." When the dog is in the Down position, the handler praises him and then quickly cancels the command. But a lot of dogs resist this method and push up their back end as soon as their handlers pull on their front legs. It's not easy for a handler to pull and push at the same time, and the dog normally goes wild.

So why not use another, easier, natural method? Let your dog sit quietly for a while, and then entice him to the ground with a dog biscuit or another treat. In this way, you can keep his rear on the ground with light pressure from your hand. Almost all dogs are interested in a snack, and with some management, a snack will help you teach your dog this exercise. With very large or heavy dogs that

Your dog must
know the Down
to perform the
Guarding Articles
exercise.

Your dog may also
need to go down
during a body
search.

haven't learned the Down in their early youth, all that "push and
pull work" of mechanical training will surely be difficult; for these
dogs, enticement works much better. Teaching the larger, stronger
breeds the Sit and Down and heelwork is of great importance. It's
best to teach them when they are still of a manageable size.

Curiosity

Most dogs, just like most people, are curious. When your young dog
is happily jumping around you and won't let himself be caught, nine
out of 10 times you can trick him into coming to you if you bend
over and touch a clump of grass, or something like that, as though

you are curious about it. Your dog will want to know what is so interesting there, and before he knows it, he is caught. This curiosity can also be used for teaching the Down. The dog has to sit, and after that you pat the ground in front of him and look as if you have discovered something special. A lot of dogs fall for this and lie down to have a better chance to sniff that place. While patting the ground, say, "Down," loud and clear to your dog. If your dog is down, reward him in that position and then quickly cancel the command.

If this method is working, patting the ground can be replaced by pointing to the ground, and later on by the command "Down." Note that it is good to cultivate the sign for down (a flat, horizontal hand). Later on in training, this sign command can be used, for instance, in a noisy place or in a situation where you have to be silent.

Waiting

All dogs can be taught to lie down because it is a natural position for them. However, it's a lot more difficult to convince your dog that he has to stay down until he gets a new command (preferably "Free"). The length of time your dog stays in the Down has to be gradually increased. The good handler observes his or her dog and knows when the best moment to cancel arrives. When the exercise goes wrong once, and the dog rises on his own, you have to ask him to go down again, after which you should fairly quickly cancel the command.

If your dog crawls from the Down position, immediately lay him down again at the starting place with a clear "Down" command. Every crawled inch has to be corrected. Remember that it is always better to keep your dog in position too short a time than too long.

Time for Training

The Down is best trained briefly a few times a day, and the best time is just before your dog gets his food. If you do this, he will quickly learn that besides all the little rewards that go with training, there

Down the decoy.

also is a big reward in the form of his full food bowl. Ask your dog to lie down when you finally give him his food bowl. After that, he is allowed to eat when you let him, with a command like "Okay" or "Take it." In this case, the Down is not only an excellent authority-confirmation exercise, but it also prevents your dog from jumping for the food bowl.

When your dog understands the "Down" command well, the period spent lying down can be gradually increased. You must, however, ensure that he is not left lying longer than he can handle. Too short a time is not a problem, but too long will never be a success, because that inevitably leads to a correction. Unnecessary corrections aren't good for any dog's enthusiasm (much less your own). Successful training has to be pleasant and interesting for both members of the team.

10

Training the Stay

In theory, but certainly not in practice, the Stay is an exercise that should not be taught separately from the Sit and Down exercises. For some handlers and their dogs, Stay is a difficult exercise. Even if a dog is very obedient, staying too long can be too much for him. This may be because of his breed, his age, his self-confidence, and even an overdeveloped bond with his handler. With enough patience, however, and perhaps a few helpers, the Stay can be taught to any dog.

When we give the command "Stay," we mean for our dogs to stay in their appointed places while we are away from them. In the beginning, you should only walk a short distance away from your dog as you practice the exercise, but the goal is to be able to walk away and stay out of your dog's sight for five or more minutes. The difficulty here is not the position of the dog but that he has to stay all alone. A young dog, especially, wants to be with his handler, and it is difficult for him to watch his handler walk away.

When you are out of sight, your dog's confidence is put to the test. So the Stay must be built up step by step, and your dog has to learn that you always come back; even when, in his opinion, it takes a long time. He must have confidence in your return, and he also must be self-confident enough to stay somewhere all alone, even in a strange place.

The Position for Stay

In general, when we talk about the Stay, we mean that the dog stays down. Surely the Down position is the most natural one for dogs. It is the position in which he rests, sleeps, and relaxes. It's important to note that once a dog is in the Down, his urge to walk away is less than it would be in Stand or Sit.

There are some examination programs that require dogs to stay sitting for some minutes. This exercise is almost always too difficult for dogs, and this advanced training is only significant as an obedience exercise, one that has no practical purpose.

There are dogs that stay better in the Sit position than the Down, and for our goal, training the protection dog, it only is important that the dog stays in his place; what position he's in is unimportant. A dog that prefers to sit or stand rather than lie down is, of course, allowed to do so, as long as he doesn't leave the appointed place.

Therefore, training young dogs to stay, which has to happen without pressure, can best be done as explained in Chapter 5,

It's not easy to stay cool after an attack like this one.

It's best for this
decoy to stay put.

"Basic Education and Exercises." For older dogs that can endure
more pressure, it's best to start training the Stay from the Down
position. If your dog doesn't like lying down, of course, the following exercise can also be done from Sit or Stand.

Step One

Before learning the Stay, dogs must first know what "Down" means
and be able to work out that exercise well. Even if you are standing
in front of your dog or are in the area as he performs the Down,
he should be able to obey the "Down" command for a few minutes
without attempting to cancel before you start teaching the Stay. Of

course, praise him exuberantly, and then ask him to "Sit," at which point you cancel the Sit with the command "Free."

When the above sequence is going well, have your dog lie down and then slowly walk a few paces backward. Stop, wait for a moment, and go back to your dog. Praise him while he is lying there. After five seconds allow him to sit, and then give him the command "Free." Together with "Free," clap your hands as an invitation to play.

For the next stage in the training, back away and then circle around your prone dog. Note that your dog will try to keep you in sight and might be tempted to turn as you circle him. It's okay if he only turns his head, but if he moves his body—crawling or turning—you need to restart the exercise. If your dog moves when you try a full circle, restart the exercise and only walk a half-circle around him.

Step Two

When your dog stays lying down as you circle around him, you know you are ready for the next step: increasing the distance between you and your dog as you back away from him. If he starts to stand up or crawl forward, you must correct him immediately and then walk away again, but not too far. Increase the distance step by step. If you and your dog are working out this stage well, try breaking off eye-contact by turning around and standing that way for a while.

In the next phases of training the Stay, turn directly around and walk away from your dog once he is in the Down, and then add more and more distance and time to the exercise. To mix it up a bit, you can also try walking away from your dog and then sitting on the ground far away from him. If something goes wrong as you advance through these stages of training, make sure you take a step back and make the exercise less difficult by decreasing the distance and time you leave your dog in the Stay.

Finishing

As always, make sure you reward your dog after each correct execution of the exercise by a simple pat on the head while he is still lying down. To correctly finish the exercise, ask your dog to sit. It can be hard for some dogs to rise from the Stay into the Sit, especially in the beginning, because they want to jump or immediately sit (before you give the command) to welcome you back. It is naturally disappointing for the dog when he gets a harsh command to go down again.

To avoid that situation, pass your dog now and then as he lies down in the Stay, but don't look at him. Because of the lack of eye contact, he will get the idea that the exercise is not finished, especially when you walk toward him and then just walk by. When you do come back to him, pet him for a few seconds as he lies there, wait about five seconds, and then give the command "Sit." When he sits correctly, allow him to play free. We think you'll find that if you don't look at your dog when you return, your dog won't jump up too early.

Out of Sight

Many dogs do excellent work in training until the moment their handlers are out of sight. Maybe they can lie still for half a minute, but then they become restless and try to sit, and some of them even take a careful look around the corner where the handler disappeared. Some dogs begin to whine, and other dogs cannot stand it anymore and run to their handlers. Teaching your dog to stay when you have disappeared, therefore, has to be built up slowly. For some dogs, it isn't a problem at all, but for excitable and attentive dogs, it's different. If your dog's character is thus, limit being out of sight to a few seconds at the beginning; if that works, increase your time out of sight to 10 seconds, and so on.

The Stay is sometimes trained in strange locations.

Remember the Little Helpers

Staying will be easier for your dog when you walk away in the direction the dog is facing; this way, he won't be tempted to turn. Sometimes it can help to leave some of your clothes near your dog as he stays—the scent of you will reassure him. The familiar odor tells the dog he has not lost his handler forever. Adding the clothes to the exercise, however, must be done in the right way, because some dogs may decide to guard the clothes.

Fastening the dog to a tie-out stake as part of training rarely has the desired effect. Most dogs are so smart that they know when they are fastened, so they don't try to walk away. For dogs that don't want to stay, only one thing will help: patiently building up the exercise step by step and constantly repeating all obedience exercises. This step-by-step build up gives dogs confidence, and regularly trained obedience exercises make obedience a habit.

Crawlers

It is annoying to have a dog that crawls away as soon as you are out of sight. He may head to an attractive clump of grass a few feet away, or he may crawl in the direction he saw you walk. Crawling away, even an inch, must be corrected by asking the dog to go down again, in the appointed place. If your dog sits and then lies down again, he will do just fine in protection dog training. Dogs that stand and stay are also okay. As long as they stay at the appointed place, there is no problem.

Every dog has something that is more difficult for him than it is for another dog; for one dog it's heelwork, for another standing and being touched, and for the third one the Stay. Remain patient and don't start the next step before your dog is working out the previous one very well. Train constantly, but not for too long at a time, and always finish with an exercise he is already working out well. This way, your dog can be rewarded, and you will always end your training sessions on a happy note.

11

Training the Stand and Touching

The exercise Stand and Allow Touching by Strangers (and also the exercise to show the teeth, for instance, to the vet) is essential for every dog and doubly so for a reliable protection dog. The perfect working out of the Stand and Touching is also the foundation for show dogs presented to the judge. It's not obvious to many dog owners that the Stand is something that, like Down and Sit, has to be taught and exercised. The Stand is useful for all dogs because every dog now and then has to go to the vet. On command, standing, allowing the touch of strangers, and even showing the teeth are things every well-educated dog should do without resistance. For some dogs, this exercise is more difficult than for others. The specific character of the breed can make this exercise problematic. Though every dog, even the most reserved or stubborn one, can fulfill the requirements for the exercise, training the dog may take a lot of patience and perseverance on the part of the handler.

No Deflated Balloon

When a vet asks a handler to have his untrained dog stand, the handler often lifts his or her dog up under his belly, and he looks like a big, hairy, deflated balloon. The result of this lift is that the dog stands, but with a lifted belly and a crooked back. The dog doesn't know what's happening to him, because what is "Stand?"

The correct way to ask your dog to stand does not involve touching him. Instead, ask him to stand up from the Sit position. Of course, this has to be taught, but it's no more difficult than teaching the Down. The difficulty with Stand comes when you start teaching your dog to stay in the Stand position.

Stand, Stay, touching by strangers, and showing the teeth aren't fun exercises for most dogs. As handlers we can try to make these exercises as pleasant as possible with rewards and encouragement. But these aren't natural exercises for dogs, and most dogs don't like these exercises until they can work them out easily, and even then they don't seem to take pleasure in them—they are at best indifferent. Because these exercises are unpleasant, dogs must be obedient to learn how to do them. The dog has to do them because we want him to, whether he enjoys them or not.

Teaching the Stand

Teaching the Stand works best when the dog starts from the Sit position. You, with your dog at your left side, step with your left leg one clear pace forward, while giving the command "Stand." Normally, your dog will do that any way without a problem, because he has learned in heelwork that heeling starts with your left leg moving forward, so he will step forward when you do and come into the stand position. However, you must prevent him from walking any further, so once he stands, turn to your dog and hold him by the collar under his chin. Let him first stand only for a few seconds, and then cancel the exercise by saying "Free" and clapping your hands and playing with him, which is his reward. Take care that your dog plays with you and not with other dogs on the training field.

When everything goes well, the amount of time your dog must stand should increase. Always ensure that he doesn't step forward, not even one pace, and that you always cancel the exercise. If he is doing well, you can try training the exercise on a sturdy table,

An alert Malinois performs the Transport exercise.

like one you might find at the vet. This helps him get used to the situation at the vet, but it also prevents him from moving since the edge of the table creates a barrier.

Follow-up

When your dog knows what "Stand" means, he can begin learning to stand at a distance from you, his handler. Teach this by gradually increasing the distance. It is best for you to stand facing your dog. In this position, your dog may be more inclined to go to you, but it is also the best position from which to correct him. If this is succeeding, you can walk around him; your dog must stay in the Stand as you walk.

As soon as the above sequence of activities is going well, add in the "touching" part of this exercise. To get him used to this, the best way to start is with you touching your dog. First walk around your dog, approach him from the front, and then touch him and pat him a bit. Lift your dog's legs apart and push on his back. If your dog is okay with all of this, play with him for a bit as a reward. After a while, train this exercise with your dog standing on a sturdy table, preferably one with a skid-proof mat.

Showing Teeth

Showing Teeth is an unpleasant exercise for dogs, but it is necessary when your dog's vet or dentist want to see his teeth or look into his mouth. We advise you to start training this exercise when your dog is a puppy.

The best way to teach the dog this exercise is in the Sit position, which causes fewer problems than the Stand. When the dog sits, close his jaws with both hands: one hand above and the other under his chin. Take care that his tongue isn't between his teeth. With the side of your thumbs, carefully lift his lips in the front, so that the vet (in training, a helper) can see the front teeth. While you lift his lips, make sure you don't scratch him with your fingernails or cover his eyes with your arms or hands. Nails in the flesh can be painful, and a hand in front of his eyes can make him feel uncertain.

The molars at the left and right side have to be examined, too, so carefully lift his lips on the sides without pushing them higher or lower than necessary. After that, your dog needs to open his mouth for an inside examination. In opening his mouth, for your own safety, always keep some flesh of his lips between your thumb and his teeth or molars to prevent him from closing his mouth.

In the beginning, it can be quite a task for your dog to show the teeth at the side of his closed mouth. When he has undergone this on one side, he should be let "Free" and rewarded. Slowly the other parts of his mouth can be shown. To make it clear to your dog what is going to happen, always say, "Show your teeth," and he will learn what this phrase means and what is required of him.

Touching by Strangers

If you start this exercise by touching your dog in the way we describe above, your dog will get used to the exercise, as long as he already knows what "Stand" means. However, when you get to the point where you are ready to allow a stranger to touch your dog, new problems may arise. For instance, most shepherds and other working-dog breeds don't like to be touched by strangers. Do not introduce a stranger into the mix until your dog can perform the Stand well, can be touched by you in the way described above, and will show his teeth in the way described above. When you do introduce the stranger, your dog needs to understand that he can only allow a stranger to touch him on your command, for example: "It's okay" or "Stay." He will never find this exercise pleasant, but he will accept it because it is your desire that he does so.

You and the stranger helper must be quiet, consistent, and confident as you train this exercise. As a transitional stage to strangers, the first helpers to touch your dog can be people he knows and loves well. Helpers and strangers alike may praise your dog for

A Bouvier des Flandres bites after an attack on his handler.

good behavior, but never allow them to reward your dog, and never let them give him treats.

Start with Young Dogs

With our own dogs, even the more reserved ones, we train the Touching by Strangers when the dogs are still young. When a dog-loving friend or another visitor drops by, we ask him or her to be the helper for this exercise. The dog has to be in the Sit or Down position, and we give him the command "It's okay" (or "Stay") while the visitor touches and carefully pats the dog. We don't allow the helper to affectionately pet or to cuddle the dog but only touch him. Petting and cuddling is reserved for the members of the family.

A Malinois uses a decoy as a climbing wall.

If all is going well so far, stand at a greater distance from your sitting, lying, or standing dog, and ask a stranger to walk quietly around your dog, which has to stay in his position. Because you are not in your dog's direct vicinity, he cannot turn to you for support, so no shuffling to you or leaning against your leg. Then, give your dog the command, and the stranger will touch him.

At first, the stranger should simply use his or her hand to quickly stroke the dog, preferably in a place where your dog can see the hand. If this goes well, the stranger can touch other places on your dog's body and limbs. During this process, your dog will become accustomed to touching by strangers. The exercise Showing the Teeth to strangers should therefore not be a problem, because in that exercise, you are the only one who touches your dog; the strangers are only allowed to look.

12

Training the Recall

If your dog knows the Recall exercise, many accidents can be prevented. It is vital that your dog come immediately when he is called. In addition, when you teach your dog the Recall, he also learns how to stay until he is called. Although dogs should be on leash around traffic, an unexpected situation can arise where your dog ends up on the other side of the street from you. Having a dog with good recall will allow you to have your dog sit, stand, or lie down until it is safe to recall him.

You can easily teach the Recall to young pups. When they walk around in the living room, we can call them several times a day and reward them with little treats. Mealtimes can also be used to teach pups to come when they are called. During their first walks, you can also call the on- or off-leash pups a few times; always reward them when they come. This way, every pup learns to come pretty quickly.

Pups that are called and don't come must not be chased and caught; they think it's fun to play, like children play tag. When they get used to this game, they don't come anymore. Teasing people to chase is, of course, more fun than coming when called. Dogs that play such naughty tricks must be systematically enticed. It may seem odd, but one way to get your tricky dog to come is to sit or even lie down. Most pups and even adult dogs will come and see what's going on when their handler is lying prone. As handlers, we have to control our impatience. Pups that come when they are called, even if it takes a while, are always "Good boys" and have to be rewarded.

Run Free

A lot of people are afraid to let their pups run free during a walk, but we let them go free as young as possible. A few days before the first walk, we teach our pups to come in the house and in the yard. The first time we let a pup run free outside is when we've had him for about one week, and we do it on a quiet, large, and preferably fenced terrain. Most of the time we also take an older dog with us, because pups imitate their elders.

In principle, a pup stays with his own pack, and that pack consists of dogs and people from his own house. A normal pup will, if he is used to his fellow pack members, stay in their vicinity. During the first free walk, we recall the pup about three times, and every time he comes, we reward him, and also the older dog(s), with a treat. In this way, he quickly learns that to be called and to come to us means good things. When he has to go on leash again, maybe coming isn't as nice, even though he is rewarded with a treat at that juncture, too. We reward with food until the dog is about one year old.

On his way down.

A police dog is always a great assistant when taking a resisting person into custody.

A lot of people are scared to let their pups run free because they are afraid they will run away. But puppies want to stay within the safety of their group. An older dog, however, which may have grown up to be an individualist, may be less insecure and more apt to wander away.

Most pups trained in the way we describe above will come when they are called. The jumpy pup or adult dog, however, can panic during a walk and stop listening. Such a dog first must learn to come as soon as possible to the leader of the pack: you. In the beginning, let a young, nervous pup run free on a thin, long leash. As soon as something startles or scares him, call him and he will come by the long leash; make sure you reward him for coming. Undesirable behavior is never rewarded, only the well-done Recall.

Correct

For some handlers, the perfect Recall looks like it will be hard to do, but it isn't so difficult. A few tricks make teaching and correctly working out the Recall exercise a lot easier. A correct performance of the Recall looks like this: At a distance from the handler, the dog is in the Sit, Down, or Stand position. After some seconds (or more) the dog is called and comes enthusiastically in a straight line to sit very close and perfectly straight in front of his handler. The dog looks up to the handler. After some seconds, either the Recall exercise is finished and the dog is "Free," or the dog is told to come to the Heel position beside the handler.

The most difficult part for most dogs is the part where they must come straight ahead and sit close to their handlers. Therefore, in the beginning, we don't command our dogs to the Heel position, because if Heel always follows the Recall, your dog will automatically sit diagonally in front of you, half way between the proper Come-fore and Heel positions. To avoid this, we train Recall to end in the Come-fore position.

Most exercises are performed more perfectly over time than they are in the beginning; the Recall is the exception. We've noted over the years that the Recall exercise is often taught and learned well in the beginning, but after some time, it becomes sloppy instead of better. One reason may be the coming to the Heel position; another, the incorrect performance of the steps necessary to get the dog to the Come-fore position quickly and perfectly straight. The handler and his dog should make a point of training for the Recall correctly, correcting even small mistakes each time.

Training the Recall

Begin training the Recall exercise by having your dog sit—or lie down or stand—when you stop. Remove his leash and back away from him. After training a while, you should be able to walk normally away from your dog (i.e., facing away). The direction you walk away from your dog is always the direction in which he is facing.

After walking a few feet—how many depends on how confidently the dog stays—stand still, facing your dog. If he attempts to walk or crawl forward, correct him by restarting the exercise.

When you stand at a certain distance in front of your dog, you can take a treat or toy out of your pocket; your dog still has to stay. Hold the treat with both hands cupped in front of your body, at your dog's eye level. The dog must still stay, even though he is, by now, very curious about what you have in your hands. After about five seconds, command "Come" or "Come-fore." The majority of dogs are now so curious that they will walk straight to their handlers. When your dog is close, lift your hands—still holding the treat—to your chest. Most dogs will sit without having to be commanded to do so.

When you are doing this for the first time with an untrained dog, you may be amazed by such quick success. Because of the treat in your hands and the lift-up trick, when your dog is in front of you, he will automatically sit because he wants to look up high at your hands and what they are holding. Later, incorrect performance of this exercise happens if you don't use both hands and the treat. When you give a reward with only the right or left hand, your dog will invariably sit diagonally to the right or the left.

Differences in Tempo

Some dogs come slowly when they are called. Most of the time they are also inclined to sit too far away from their handlers. If you want to know how far away your dog should be when he sits, he should be close enough that you can touch him without having to bend over. If you want to encourage your slow dog, take one or (in the beginning) more steps backward before he arrives at the location where he should sit. If you do this, your dog will come closer to you.

On the other side of the spectrum, there are enthusiastic dogs that find the Recall a fantastic game, and they will run to and almost climb their handlers, or at least collide with them. This enthusiasm is often accompanied by an excited bark, or a jump up to the handler's face. When such a dog immediately sits correctly after that initial wildness, there is no problem. The dog must not be punished for his happiness. If the collision or jumping becomes too much of a problem, such as a large dog that knocks his handler over, the handler can jut out his knee, which often solves the problem. After exercising for some time, the dog's over-enthusiasm will quiet down.

A Pleasant Exercise

Unlike Stand and Show Teeth, the Recall is a pleasant exercise for most dogs. The excitement of the duty to stay until called makes them attentive. We get the impression that a lot of dogs view it as a kind of game. They learn to stay attentive and to listen well because the reward follows when they have performed the exercise correctly. A dog that still can't handle staying alone can be held by a helper until the handler recalls him. After keeping him on a stretched leash, he can be held on a slack leash, and later on with only a loose leash over his back. Slowly, the dog will understand the Recall exercise.

Although the rattan stick breaks from the hit, the dog knows his duty.

In daily life, the Recall is a useful exercise that has to be performed several times a day. With our dogs we have a difference between the official and correct Recall and the daily "coming." In the latter case, we call the dog by his name and say, "Okay, come on," or "Okay, come here," which means come to us, because we have to put on the leash or we have to remove twigs from his coat or any other interaction. In this mundane version of the Recall, our dogs know that they don't have to sit in front of us; if necessary, we can give them the proper command for that. Our dogs quickly understand the distinction between the correct Recall and the daily "coming." In making this distinction, we also take care that the correct Recall doesn't get lost through careless training. It's the same difference as that between Heel and "not pulling the leash," as we note in our thoughts on heelwork.

13

Training the Send Away

Probably the most difficult exercise for advanced dogs is the Send Away. A dog that has been in training for a while has built up a strong bond with his handler. He is attentive to everything the handler does and says, and he reacts immediately to the commands or signs. But, when the Send Away exercise is added to the program, many dogs are confused when they are expected to go away from their handlers in a straight line. Normally, the dog has to be in the handler's vicinity, to do as fast as he can all the things the handler asks for. For a lot of dogs, therefore, the Send Away is a big problem. In the eyes of the dog, it is a nonsense exercise: he is sent away, only to be recalled fairly quickly.

Indeed, the Send Away, from the dog's perspective, is just a run straight ahead for a certain distance, mostly followed by a "Down" command that he knows will be followed shortly by a Recall. So, it's a bit of an inconsistent-looking exercise for him. Dogs that know what the Send Away means will sometimes lie down on their own at a certain distance or look back at the handler, waiting for the command.

We see the same problem with some experienced police dogs that know the Recall of the Pursuing Dog, an important and often difficult exercise in the protection phase. In this exercise the dog

The dog comes in at a great speed and grabs hold at the last moment.

is sent after a fleeing decoy. Within 164 feet (50 m) of the decoy, the handler recalls the dog. We sometimes see such dogs look over their shoulder at about this distance, to be sure that the handler doesn't forget the recall command. Note that as long as they continue running at the same tempo as the decoy, they normally will not lose points for this behavior at a trial.

Of course, it is your task as handler to avoid such automatism as much as possible. Changing the lessons to include many different endings prevents smart dogs from lying down or coming back on their own, thinking the distance was far enough.

Down at a Distance

Since dogs have to lie down after the Send Away, it is good to teach them to drop on command from a distance before training the Send Away. A dog that doesn't react to the "Down" command from a distance won't be able to learn the Send Away. It is, of course, essential for you to be able to command your dog to "Down" quickly, without having to coerce him.

Begin by teaching your dog to lie down on command immediately when he is at a short distance from you. We start by training the exercise on leash. Let your dog walk around for a bit, and when he is a certain distance away, suddenly command "Down." He may refuse or want to come back to you; but you must prevent this (see Different Methods below). Try to train this exercise in different places and conditions, so that your dog understands and responds quickly to your command in a variety of locales. He must lie down until you give him the command "Free," or stand beside him and with the command "Sit" allow him to heel in the beginning position. At first, don't call your dog to you.

If your dog lies down on command at the limit of the leash, then next time drop the leash on the ground when he lies down on command. After that, teach him to lie down four feet (1 m) away without the leash. If this works, gradually increase the distance and length of time your dog lies down.

Different Methods

To avoid problems with the Send Away, it is good to give the exercise a point. Depending on the type of dog you have, there are different correct working methods for training the exercise. For instance, most shepherd dogs like to stay as close as possible to their handlers; for them a distance of 16 feet (5 m) is far enough. Sadly for them, 16 feet is not far enough for the Send Away; they really have to learn to go on forward in the direction indicated. This can be done by sending them to something lying or standing at the end of the terrain. With our dogs, we place a worn T-shirt (or coat) in a specific location, and after our command they can go into the Down position close to, or at, the article of clothing.

In another method, we use a bite pillow or a sleeve. Place the pillow 26 to 33 feet (8 to 10 m) in front of the dog, and if everything goes well, decrease that distance gradually. In the beginning, the dog may catch the bite pillow and bring it to his handler to play together. Later on, we can first command the dog to lie down near the bite pillow and then come to the handler to play together.

For one particular dog, one method is better; for another dog, another system is more successful. Other items you might use to teach the Send Away include food, clothes, white blocks, plastic cones, or articles the dog loves.

Teaching Go Out

First, your dog has to learn the meaning of the command for the Send Away, which can be "Go," "Go out," or "Go on." You can teach this exercise to your young dog by sending him from a distance to his food bowl and repeating the command several times. In a short time, he will know what that command means, and he will also go farther away from you, his handler.

When your dog knows the command, the next steps are to first send him to a food bowl with only a small treat in it; then send him to a bowl with nothing in it, but as soon as he is at the bowl, recall him and give him a treat. Training this exercise in this way is pleasant for your dog. If you are training an adult dog, make sure he knows what "Go out" means before starting training on the field.

STEPS TO A STRONG SEND AWAY

Send Away means that the dog runs on in the direction indicated until he receives another command. To promote this going on far

It is impossible to escape this dog.

away, it is good to allow your dog to always run to the end of the terrain, until he comes up against a barrier such as a fence, wall, or ditch. There, you have already placed a marked point (sometimes with a treat), a piece of clothing, or a toy. Even if the distance of the Send Away is not great the first few times (depending on the speed of the dog), the goal should always be the end of the terrain. Dogs that think the send away is a bit of free time and that try to walk away can be corrected by a long line. They will be sent forward fastened on a 50-foot (15-m) (or more) line. The next step is to send them away with a normal leash trailing loosely behind them, and if this is successful, the leash is taken away.

The first part of the Send Away is your dog sitting at heel. Ensure he is in a perfect starting position and show him the direction he needs to go by directing his head and making him attentive. To do this, you can ask a helper to position him or herself at the end of the terrain, standing behind the point (with or without the supports) where the dog has to go to in a straight line. Then say, "Go out," step forward, and show with an outstretched arm the direction in which he has to go. Give the command with energy and power. This gives the dog verbal encouragement. At first, your dog will probably only go a short distance and then turn around, hoping you will give instructions about what has to happen next. Point in the right direction again and repeat the command. At the same time, your helper should call your dog.

Many handlers use a treat at the end, set at a marked point, which can also work when training older dogs. After a few times, your dog knows what is meant by "Go out," and you must change the reward at this point, so that there won't always be a treat on the marked point at the end. A possible disadvantage to the change will be that while he is searching for the treat, he may not hear your "Down" command.

This problem with treats is why we employ the worn piece of clothing we mentioned above. We also send our dogs out in different directions, but always to the end of the field. In the first

A Back Transport of two decoys.

training sessions, your dog may look while you are laying the treat/clothing down at the end of the terrain, but later on, ask a helper to do this, and later still ensure that your dog doesn't know where the item is. Our dogs are always happy when they find something with our odor on it, and this is their stimulus to quickly do this exercise.

14

Practical Obedience

In this chapter, we will talk about some common situations that can prove to be dangerous or uncomfortable for poorly trained dogs. These situations come up during day-to-day activities. After training the exercises in all the preceding chapters, your dog may know his tasks very well, but remember that practice makes perfect. During training, your dog's heelwork, Sit, Down, Stand, and Recall may be perfect, but in daily practice it may look like he's forgotten these important exercises. Here are some tips to help you put all this knowledge to work in real life.

Commands Are Orders

During grooming, it is helpful when your dog does not repeatedly turn around, sit, and lie down in the way he wants. It is always easier if your dog does as you command. So "Stand" during grooming means stay standing, "Sit" means stay sitting, and for "Down," he must lie down. Whether the dog likes it or not is not up for discussion. Commands are in force, even under the shower and in the vet's surgery. Attempts to flee, growls, and other misbehavior are absolutely not allowed. The command is an order and has to be obeyed. Maybe with very young dogs you don't have to be so strict, but even pups can't act up, menace, or panic. Quietly, but convincingly, help your dog sit or stand when he cannot (or will not) do it on his own.

Many people leave the cutting of their dogs' nails to a groomer or a vet because they are afraid to cause their dogs pain. But there are also people who know, or think, that their dogs will not allow the cutting. This, of course, should not happen; you should be able to touch, inspect, and groom your dog, and even be able to cut his nails. Maybe your dog doesn't really like it, but it still has to happen. Command your dog "Down," and tell him to stay in that position while cutting his nails. Of course, when this is finished, play with him for a while to show it wasn't so bad after all.

Going Outside

When it's time to go outside in the morning, your dog already knows something he likes very much is going to happen. Pleased, he jumps up on you because there is an outing on the program. Many handlers then have to struggle to get their dogs on leash, sometimes swinging the leash to lasso their dogs. With some excitable dogs, this "dog catching" can be quite a job.

However, this is a good opportunity to put "Sit" into daily practice. Teach your dog, preferably from a young age, that you only put on the

During the Side Transport exercise, the dog must be alert for any incriminating objects the "suspect" might drop.

leash, so he can go outside, when he quietly sits. To make this a correct habit, the command "Sit" has to be given, after which your dog sits on his own, or with your help (and a treat). It will not take long before he understands and will sit by himself, ready to be leashed. The same has to happen outside. After walking off leash and coming back to you, he always has to be leashed in the Sit position.

FIRST OUT THE DOOR

Once your dog is on leash and you open the door, he runs for it, pulling you against the doorframe and down the stairs. I'm sure most of you have found yourself in this situation. To prevent stretched arms, stumbling, and pushing, teach your dog that you always go first through the doorway or gate. At doors and gates that open inward, ensure your dog learns to take a few steps back, and after that he may go beside or behind you through the opening. In the beginning, training your dog to go through doors and gates is, of course, easier when these open outward.

Your dog also must learn to walk quietly with you through revolving doors. This should work out well if he already knows that you go first and he must walk diagonally behind you, with his nose positioned alongside your leg.

Staircases

You have to teach your dog to walk quietly up and down stairs. Going up stairs, most dogs run ahead of the handler. Being pulled up the stairs by a leashed dog can be an advantage, but being pulled down the stairs can be very dangerous. When walking up or down narrow stairs or on a narrow path, it is good to teach the dog to walk with his head beside us and his body angled behind us. To accomplish this, use the command "Behind," "Back," or "Rear." At first, keep him on leash. Put the leash between your legs and keep your dog in his place behind you whenever he moves to walk beside you; if you have to, use your hands to push or tap him backward. It is good to train this in narrow passages, or close beside a wall on your left side, where your dog can't come to heel. This command also comes in handy when walking through a mass of people.

In the Car

Getting into a car is generally no problem for a dog that likes to travel. There are even dogs that like to sit in parked cars. During a drive, a protection dog has to lie down in the back seat of the car, or down in the open back space of a hatchback or station wagon. He has to stay there without trying to climb forward because a dog that comes to the front while the car is in motion is a serious danger. To teach him to stay back, in the beginning, you should have another person in the car with you. The helper can keep an eye on the dog and hold him back when he tries to come into the front of the car. The punishment for this behavior must come from you, the handler: command your dog in a firm, harsh tone to "Stay" (or "Down"), with the helper physically preventing him from moving.

Your dog has to lie down in the car: sitting or standing is not allowed. Standing is the first step toward moving forward. If in the teaching phase there is no helper in the car, fasten your dog securely in the back seat or in the back space. This is only a security

This dog keeps the decoy stationary by biting his leg.

precaution for you, the driver, because your dog has to learn to stay by command in his appointed place. Some people allow their dogs to lie down in front of the front passenger seat, but this place is only suitable for quiet and confident dogs.

Out of the Car

Some dogs lose their lives by jumping out of the car. In the beginning, your dog will try to come out of the car on his own. But he must immediately be picked up and put back in his place with a harsh "No" (or "Stop it"), followed by a more quiet "Sit."

It's important that you instead ensure your dog comes out of the car in a fixed, special way, which should become a ritual. Dogs are animals of habit, and when they learn a certain procedure, they will soon not stray from that procedure. A safe method to prevent your dog from jumping out of the car is, after opening the door, first taking your dog's leash. During the drive your dog should have his leash fastened to his collar, or after the car stops, you should fasten the leash before either of you get out of the car. While all the people in the car get out, your dog should learn to stay in the car in the Down or Sit. After you pick up his leash and give him a command, your dog may leave the car.

Coming in at a great speed, this dog jumps high to bite the decoy.

In this way, your dog learns that, although the side doors or hatchback are open, he has to stay inside until his leash is picked up and he gets the command. On a quiet street, you can train this easily. The commands are "Sit" (or "Down"), and when you take up the leash (and not a second earlier), say your dog's name and "Okay, come" (or something like that). If your dog is trained in a secure and correct way, even in varying circumstances, he will become a confident traveler, no longer in a panic to jump out of the car.

Protection

15

The Dutch Police Dog Test

Before we describe the work and attitude of the decoy and the training of the protection dog, we'd like to mention some different training programs for bite work. In the Schutzhund program, which is now the IPO program, you only have to perform the bite work with the sleeve. You can find out more about this interesting training program in our book *K9 Schutzhund Training*, also published by Brush Education, Inc.

Decoys usually encourage dogs to bite their sleeve rather than another part of the body. For instance, in the Attack from a Distance, many decoys have the habit of keeping their sleeved arm in front of their body to catch the dog. Of course, the dog can still attack the legs, and in certain programs, like Ringsport, that will be taught from the beginning.

When the dog attacks the decoy on the leg, the decoy must take more care in how he touches with the stick than he would if the dog was attacking the sleeve. An attack on the legs can also distract the decoy, who is trying to keep his balance, and can lead to misplaced hits on the dog.

In the French and Belgian Ringsport programs, we mainly see bite work performed on the leg of the decoy, and in the program of the Royal Dutch Police Dog Association (KNPV), as described in this chapter, the dog can, in some exercises, bite on arms and legs. These police dogs often demonstrate very nice bite work in pursuing a decoy or in apprehending a decoy who flees on a bicycle.

K9 protection training is based on the dog protecting and defending the dog's handler, the handler's family, friends, and their possessions, but the training is also helpful when we wish to identify and arrest offenders. Dogs that train for police work in the Netherlands undergo a system prepared by the Royal Dutch Police Dog Association (in Dutch: *Koninklijke Nederlandse Politiehond Vereniging* [KNPV]), founded 1907. The training of police dogs in other countries is mostly based on this Dutch method, although in several countries there are differences in the implementation. Therefore, it makes sense for us to include an overview of the Dutch police dog training here and explain the different exercises included in that program.

Police Dog 1

The certificate Police Dog 1 (PH-1) is the standard certificate for the modern police dog. There also is a Police Dog 2 (PH-2) certificate issued to the advanced police dog, specific for the top class.

Dogs participating in the test should be at least two years old and must have a minimum shoulder height of about 22 inches (55 cm). Dogs should preferably not exceed a shoulder height of 28 inches (70 cm). The dogs must have good teeth and a good coat, and they must generally meet the requirements for a healthy, burly, adult dog. Dogs belonging to one of the following varieties are allowed for certification: sheepdog (in all its varieties), Doberman, giant schnauzer, Bouvier des Flandres, Airedale terrier, Rottweiler, boxer, and all crosses between these breeds. Pit-bull terriers and their crosses are excluded from tests, as are dogs with docked ears and/or tail. Dogs that suffer from any disease or that are visibly pregnant are not admitted to the tests, either. Also, if the handler cannot vouch for the reliability of his or her dog, he or she may not participate in the test.

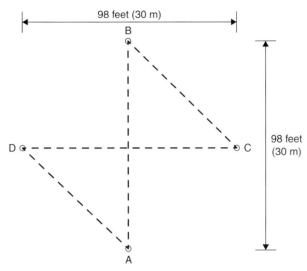

As instructed by the judge, the handler must follow this diabolo pattern with his dog from A to B to C to D and then back to A.

The certification test for PH-1 consists of three parts. Part 1 covers the common skills, such as the dog's basic obedience and control; Part 2 covers specific skills for water work; and Part 3 tests the protection exercises. Besides these parts, there are two parts of "general outlook," one for the dog (general obedience) and one for the handler (the way the handler presents his or her dog at the test).

PART 1

A. HEELING ON LEASH: 5 POINTS

This is the only exercise during the test where the dog is on a leash. Handler and leashed dog follow a diabolo diagram that is plotted by cones. The first and third legs are about 98 feet (30 m) long; the second and fourth about 49 feet (15 m).

B. HEELING WITHOUT A LEASH, AT THE RIGHT AND LEFT SIDE: 5 POINTS

Here, handler and dog follow the same diabolo diagram as in the on-leash heeling. At the first diagonal side, the handler instructs the dog to move from the left side to the right, and at the second diagonal side, the handler instructs the dog to move back to the left side, at the command of the judge. The patterns involve right and left turns, stops and about-turns that are similar to basic obedience routines. The heeling is not as precise as it is in Schutzhund trials but rather is somewhat loose. The main objective in this exercise is to follow a line. Few points are lost in this phase, regardless of precision.

C. HEELING NEXT TO A BICYCLE: 5 POINTS

The bicycle heeling is an extension of the walking phase, by which the handler and dog follow the same diabolo pattern as in the first two exercises. The dog must follow closely, always at the handler's right side, right next to the bike, even when the handler at the beginning and end of the exercise must walk beside the bicycle. The dog is not allowed to walk in front or behind, or too far away from the handler during any of the heeling exercises (A, B, and C).

D. DOWN STAY: 5 POINTS

The handler instructs the dog to stay down at a spot appointed by the judge and leaves the dog for three minutes, going to a hiding place out of the dog's sight.

E. REFUSAL OF OFFERED AND THROWN FOOD: 5 POINTS

The handler instructs the dog to stay down at a spot appointed by the judge, and at a signal given by the judge, leaves the dog to stay down. Subsequently, the decoy approaches in front of the dog. At about 16 feet (5 m) in front of the dog, the decoy shows the dog some food, keeping his hands at waist level. Then the decoy offers two pieces of food to the dog with his left and right hand, one hand at a time. The food should not be pushed against the nose or the mouth of the dog. If the dog refuses, the decoy drops the food. He then walks backward, and from a distance of 6.5 to 10 feet (2–3 m), he throws a third piece of food toward but not at the dog. Then the decoy moves away from the dog.

The food refusal exercise is rather unique in that a full-suited decoy offers and throws food in front of the dog. This exercise requires a great deal of self-control and restraint on the part of the dog because it is the only exercise in which the decoy is not presented as a target for attack. The exercise requires that the dog not take or touch the food. She must stay and not attack the decoy. If during this exercise the dog bites the decoy, he may only offer food or throw it after the dog has released him.

F. REFUSAL OF FOUND FOOD: 5 POINTS
For this exercise, food is scattered in a few different places over the area on which the heeling, staying down, and jumping takes place. During this exercise, the dog is not allowed to take or lick the food.

G. BE SILENT: 5 POINTS
This exercise is a temperament test, of sorts. It requires that the dog and handler stay quietly in the woods after, following a sign from the judge, a group of people play-act an altercation and a 9 mm pistol is fired at a distance of about 66 feet (20 m). To receive maximum points, the dog must not bark or yelp.

H. FREE JUMP OVER A THREE-FOOT (1-M) -HIGH HEDGE: 5 POINTS
The handler instructs the dog to jump over an obstacle that is three feet (1 m) high. The dog should go back and forth over the obstacle at the commands of her handler, without actually touching the obstacle.

I. JUMP OVER A 5.7-FOOT (1.75-M) -HIGH WALL: 5 POINTS
Here the dog has to jump over a 5.7-foot (1.75-m) -high straight wall with a slope and stay on the other side of the wall.

J. JUMP OVER A 10-FOOT- (3-M) -LONG, 7.4-FOOT (2.25-M) -WIDE, AND 3-FOOT (1-M) -DEEP DITCH: 5 POINTS
The dog has to jump back and forth over the ditch at the command of her handler.

K. SEARCHING FOR AND RETRIEVING SMALL ARTICLES: 15 POINTS
  1. *Manner of searching*   *6 points*
  2. *Way of retrieving*   *9 points*

This last exercise in Part 1 is the article search. It is a practical exercise designed to be used by police in the field. It is used to

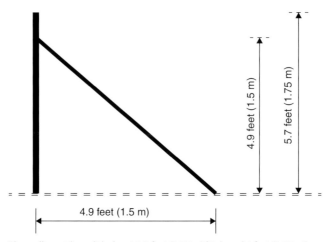

4.9 feet (1.5 m)

4.9 feet (1.5 m)

5.7 feet (1.75 m)

The wall must be solid, about 5.7 feet (1.75 m) high and 4 feet (1.25 m) wide. The back side of the wall, about 10 inches (25 cm) below the top, should have a non-slippery slope of the same width as the wall at an angle of 45 degrees.

recover stolen property or evidence of a crime. The dog is given seven minutes to search for three small objects in a mowed, grassy area that is 46 × 46 feet (14 × 14 m). The search area should be marked off with piles of soil, sod, or edges of lime. The articles can include objects such as a small ring, a key, or a button; the articles must be covered in human odor and be made of materials that can't be chewed by the dog. One of the objects must be an open cartridge case of a pistol or revolver having a diameter of 0.35 inches (9 mm) and a length of 0.75 inches (19 mm). The dog is graded according to the intensity of her search, the manner in which she searches, and the quality of her retrieve.

PART 2

The Netherlands is a low and wet country divided by thousands of canals. It therefore makes sense that an exercise of the type below should be included in a trial for police dogs operating in the Netherlands. The exercise is very practical, especially the part where the dog is required to retrieve a large object.

A. SWIMMING ACROSS A 49-FOOT (15-M) -WIDE CANAL: 10 POINTS
  1. *Waiting and obeying command*   *5 points*
  2. *Way of swimming*   *5 points*

The dog should swim across a canal (minimum width 49 feet [15 m]) as instructed by her handler. The dog should wait on the other side of the canal and should swim back to the handler when commanded to do so.

B. RETRIEVING A LARGE OBJECT OUT OF THE WATER: 10 POINTS
  1. *Waiting and obeying command*   *5 points*
  2. *Way of retrieving*   *5 points*

At the handler's command, the dog should retrieve an object that floats approximately 23 feet (7 m) from the shore and bring it ashore to her handler. The object is a shelf, three feet (1 m) long, four inches (10 cm) wide, and 0.79 inches (2 cm) thick, of white or another light color, with a slat in the middle on both sides. This retrieving can be useful in the recovery of evidence.

During the swimming phase, the dog is scored according to the manner in which she swims (i.e., how fast and how straight a line she swims to cross the 49-foot (15-m) -wide canal and return). She is also scored on her obedience to her handler's commands. The same applies to the dog's retrieval of the object. Once retrieved, the dog must drag it up to the handler, and it must be brought to the judge by the dog or her handler.

PART 3

A. GUARDING AN ARTICLE: 10 POINTS
  1. *Way of guarding*   *5 points*
  2. *Sharpness during the guarding* *5 points*

The handler positions the dog at a spot appointed by the judge and places an article there for the dog to guard. The article is 18 × 12 inches (45 cm × 30 cm), something like a briefcase or suit coat. At a sign from the judge, the handler leaves the dog to stay down for three minutes. Subsequently, the decoy passes the dog at a distance of 6.5 feet (2 m). After he has gone about 33 feet (10 m) past the dog, the decoy turns around, walks toward the dog and the article, and tries to pick up the article. The dog should not allow the decoy to pick the article up or take it away. She must bite as soon as the decoy has come within 6.5 feet (2 m) of her.

B. SEARCHING FOR A LARGE OBJECT HIDDEN IN THE WOODS: 25 POINTS

1. *Waiting and obeying command*   *5 points*
2. *Way of searching*   *5 points*
3. *Barking*   *5 points*
4. *Guarding*   *5 points*
5. *Not biting the object*   *5 points*

In a partly overgrown area measuring 492 × 246 feet (150 × 75 m), the dog has to search for a wooden box that is 18 × 12 × 6 inches (45 × 30 × 15 cm), which the judge hid shortly before the start of the exercise. When the dog has found the box, she should bark continuously and is not allowed to bite into the box. The dog has seven minutes to complete this exercise; however, if she has not found the box within three minutes, points are deducted.

C. SEARCHING FOR A PERSON HIDDEN IN THE WOODS: 25 POINTS

1. *Waiting and obeying command*   *5 points*
2. *Way of searching*   *5 points*
3. *Barking*   *5 points*
4. *Guarding*   *5 points*
5. *Not biting the person*   *5 points*

In an area measuring 492 × 246 feet (150 × 75 m), the dog has to search for a decoy standing still, who has been hidden by the judge shortly before the exercise started. When the dog has found the decoy, she should guard him and bark continuously. After approximately 10 barks, the decoy attempts by one softly spoken command and two loud commands to stop the dog from guarding him. The dog should not fall silent; she may, however, bite in response but immediately "Out" by herself when the decoy stops shouting. The dog should continue to bark until her handler joins her. The dog has seven minutes to find the person; however, as with the hidden object in the previous exercise, if she has not found him within three minutes, points are deducted.

D. TRANSPORT OF AN ARRESTED MAN: 15 POINTS

1. *Way of transportation*   5 *points*
2. *Not biting during transport*   5 *points*
3. *Retrieving a dropped metal article* 5 *points*

The dog and her handler transport the decoy over a distance of about 164 feet (50 m). After 66 feet (20 m), the decoy drops out of his left armpit a set of keys that the dog immediately should pick up and retrieve to her handler. After a further 66 feet of normal transport, the decoy enacts walking under the influence of alcohol for another 66 feet; this is followed by 33 feet (10 m) of normal transport.

E. APPREHENDING A SUSPECT WHO DEFENDS HIMSELF WITH A STICK: 35 POINTS

1. *Waiting and obeying command*   5 *points*
2. *Way of pursuit*   5 *points*
3. *Way of apprehending*   5 *points*
4. *Firmness regarding the stick* 5 *points*
5. *Out*   5 *points*
6. *Not biting*   5 *points*
7. *Guarding*   5 *points*

In this exercise, the decoy tests the dog's fear of threats and the stick and how the dog apprehends a defendant. When the decoy walks into view in the middle of the terrain and raises his stick, the handler calls out, "Halt, police!" twice. After that, the decoy starts to run. The handler commands the dog to stop the decoy. When the dog is approximately 82 feet (25 m) away from the starting point, the judge fires a gun, which is also a sign for the handler to follow the dog as quickly as possible to the location where the command to release must be issued. Following the gunfire, the decoy disappears from the view of both the dog and the handler. When the dog is within 82 feet (25 m) of the decoy, the decoy turns around quickly and tries to stop the dog from attacking by giving threatening commands; the decoy also administers one tolerable hit with the stick. The decoy advances in a natural position toward the dog, makes threatening upward movements with the stick, and keeps his other arm slightly bent or next to his body, making himself look as wide as possible. The stick stroke should not land on the dog's legs or head, but should contact from back to front on the dog's back. The dog must bite the decoy's leg, otherwise her points for the exercise are deducted. After the command of her handler to release, "Out," the dog has to guard the decoy.

Here a dog apprehends a suspect who defends himself with a stick (here, just broken).

F. REFUSING TO OBEY COMMANDS GIVEN BY A SUSPECT: 20 POINTS

1. *Refusing commands*   *5 points*
2. *Out*   *5 points*
3. *Not biting*   *5 points*
4. *Guarding*   *5 points*

After the attack and the Out in the former exercise, the decoy drops his stick and attempts by different commands to stop the dog from guarding him. The dog is scored according to whether or not she responds to the decoy's threatening commands. She is allowed to bite but does not have to.

G. TRANSPORT FOLLOWED BY APPREHENDING A FLEEING SUSPECT: 30 POINTS

1. *Way of transportation*   *5 points*
2. *Not biting during transport* *5 points*
3. *Way of apprehending*   *5 points*
4. *Out*   *5 points*
5. *Not biting*   *5 points*
6. *Guarding*   *5 points*

After exercise F, the handler and dog transport the decoy over a distance of approximately 82 feet (25 m). Then the decoy turns around and runs away from the handler and dog in the direction they were coming from. The dog should, without a command or sign, immediately stop the decoy. When the decoy stands still, the handler instructs the dog to release the decoy, and the handler goes to the dog and leads her away, off leash, for 82 feet (25 m).

H. APPREHENDING A SUSPECT WHO FLEES ON A BICYCLE: 30 POINTS

1. *Waiting and obeying command* *5 points*
2. *Way of pursuit*   *5 points*
3. *Way of apprehending*   *5 points*
4. *Out*   *5 points*
5. *Not biting*   *5 points*
6. *Guarding*   *5 points*

This dog
refuses to obey
commands given
by a "suspect."

The next attack involves the dog pursuing a fleeing bicyclist. The decoy walks into view of both the dog and her handler. The handler shouts, "Halt, police!" once, but the decoy gets on his bicycle and cycles away in view of the handler. The handler shouts, "Halt, police!" once more and then commands the dog to pursue the fleeing decoy. When the dog is 82 feet (25 m) away from the start point, the decoy disappears from the view of both dog and handler. When the dog has advanced to within 16 to 23 feet (5–7 m) of the decoy, the decoy increases his speed. The dog must bite the decoy's leg to stop him, otherwise her points for that exercise are deducted. After this, the decoy steps off his bicycle and walks some paces away with the dog maintaining her hold, and then the decoy stands still. The handler, who has followed the dog and is now approximately 98 feet (30 m) away, commands the dog to release.

The dog must bite the decoy's leg to stop him from fleeing on his bike.

I. APPREHENDING A FLEEING SUSPECT: 20 POINTS

1. *Way of apprehending*   *5 points*

2. *Out*   *5 points*

3. *Not biting*   *5 points*

4. *Guarding*   *5 points*

At a sign from the judge, the decoy flees in the direction indicated by the judge. Without a command or sign from the handler, the dog has to apprehend the fleeing suspect by biting. Then the decoy stands still and the handler has to command the dog to release and guard the decoy. At a sign from the judge, the handler goes to the dog.

J. APPREHENDING A SUSPECT WHO SHOOTS WITH A GUN: 35 POINTS

1. *Waiting and obeying command*   *5 points*

2. *Way of pursuit*   *5 points*

3. *Way of apprehending*   *5 points*

4. *Firmness regarding the shooting*   *5 points*

5. *Out*   *5 points*

6. *Not biting*   *5 points*

7. *Guarding*   *5 points*

When the decoy comes into view, he fires a gun in the direction of the handler and the dog. The handler shouts, "Halt, police!" twice and commands the dog to pursue. When the dog is 82 feet (25 m) away from the starting point, the decoy disappears from the view of both dog and handler. When the dog has come to within 82 feet (25 m) of the decoy, the decoy fires another shot in the dog's direction and drops the gun. The dog must bite the decoy's leg to stop him, otherwise her points for that exercise are deducted. If the dog stops the decoy correctly, he walks on for another 16 to 23 feet (5–7 m) to see if the dog has grabbed him properly. After that, the decoy turns around toward the handler who has followed the dog and is now at a distance of about 98 feet (30 m), ready to command the dog to release.

K. TESTING THE DOG REGARDING OBJECTS THROWN AT THE DOG: 20 POINTS

1. *Firmness regarding throwing*   *5 points*
2. *Out*   *5 points*
3. *Not biting*   *5 points*
4. *Guarding*   *5 points*

When the decoy comes into view, he fires a gun in the direction of the handler and dog.

The objects used in this exercise are thin rubber hoses, 6 to 10 inches (15–25 cm) long and 1 inch (3 cm) in diameter. At a sign from the judge, the decoy picks up an object to throw. The dog should respond immediately by attacking the decoy. The decoy then throws the object onto the dog's back. This is repeated twice, after which the decoy stops the assault and holds still. The handler commands the dog "Out" and walks toward the dog, who should at this point be guarding the decoy.

L. TRANSPORT FOLLOWED BY DEFENDING THE HANDLER: 30 POINTS
1. *Way of transportation*   *5 points*
2. *Not biting during transport*   *5 points*
3. *Way of defending*   *5 points*
4. *Out*   *5 points*
5. *Not biting*   *5 points*
6. *Guarding*   *5 points*

As soon as the handler reaches the dog, he or she starts the Transport. After 82 feet (25 m) of walking, the decoy attacks the handler. Without a sign or command, the dog should respond immediately by attacking the decoy and defending her handler. After a short wrestle, the decoy ceases the attack, and the handler walks about 6.5 feet (2 m) away from him and commands the dog "Out." As soon as the dog by itself or on command releases the decoy, the handler goes behind a judge so that the dog's guarding methods can be observed once more.

M. RECALL OF THE PURSUING DOG: 15 POINTS
1. *Waiting and obeying commands*   *5 points*
2. *Way of pursuit*   *5 points*
3. *Way of coming back*   *5 points*

An important and often difficult phase of testing is the Recall. In this exercise, the dog is sent after a fleeing decoy. When she is about 65 feet (20 m) from the starting point of the decoy, the handler recalls the dog. The dog is scored according to the manner of

During the Transport, the decoy attacks the handler, and the dog immediately defends him or her.

her pursuit, the precision of her recall, and the speed at which she returns to her handler.

N. APPREHENDING A FLEEING PERSON WHO SURRENDERS IN TIME, FOLLOWED BY A TRANSPORT: 20 POINTS

1. *Waiting and obeying command*   *5 points*
2. *Way of pursuit*   *5 points*
3. *Guarding*   *5 points*
4. *Way of transportation*   *5 points*

In this exercise, also called the Feigned Attack, a judge tests the dog on her ability to refrain from biting a suspect who stands still before being transported. When the decoy walks into view of dog and handler and raises his stick, the handler calls out, "Halt, police!"

twice. The decoy immediately starts running, after which the dog is given the command to stop the decoy. When the dog is 82 feet (25 m) from the decoy's starting point, the decoy disappears from view of both dog and handler. When the dog has come to within approximately 132 feet (40 m) of the decoy, the decoy turns around, crosses his arms, faces the dog, drops the stick, and stands still. When the dog arrives at the decoy, she should not bite or else the exercise will be terminated and the dog won't receive any points. Instead, the dog has to guard the decoy without touching him. At a sign from the judge, the handler walks toward the dog and stops 6.5 feet (2 m) behind the decoy. The handler then signals the decoy to start the Transport. During the Transport, the handler and dog remain at a distance of 6.5 feet (2 m) behind the decoy. After walking for 82 feet (25 m), the judge instructs the handler to stop the Transport.

Points

POINTS TOTAL

Part 1	65
Part 2	20
Part 3	330
General obedience	10
Way of presenting	10
Maximum score	435

MINIMUM POINTS FOR CERTIFICATE

The dog must receive 348 points to receive her certificate, and she must receive at least the following number of points in the following parts of the test:

Part 1:	40
Part 3: Exercises B and C	24
Part 3: Exercise E	18
Part 3: Exercise H	15
Part 3: Exercise J	18

During the Transport, the handler and dog remain at a distance of about 6.5 feet (2 m) behind the decoy.

The Police Dog 1 (PH-1) is the standard certificate for the modern police dog.

To receive a certificate *met lof* ("with praise"), the dog must receive a total of 392 points and all attack exercises must be excellent.

Guidelines for KNPV Decoys, Dogs, and Handlers

The decoy guidelines of the KNPV testing regulations include the following instructions and requirements.

- The decoy must be in good physical condition.

- His leather suit must provide adequate protection during bite work. The jute bite suit should be complete and of dark color. He should wear high, sturdy, closed leather shoes without studs. Leather strips may be under the soles of the shoes.

- He is always in contact with the judge during the execution of the exercises, especially in unusual situations.

- In all cases, he ensures his escape path is directed away from the handler.

- He moves as little as possible if standing still; this must be carried out until the handler and dog have been removed 82 feet (25 m) from him or the dog is on leash.

- During all transports, he walks in an ordinary way, without excessive arm movements, except during exercise D, Transport of an Arrested Man, in the part where he enacts walking under the influence of alcohol.

- The sticks he uses are normal, unpeeled, rattan sticks.

  Furthermore, the decoy should know that:

- Signs by the judge are given to him with the scorebook.

- For all exercises he receives instructions from the judge.

- Phrases such as generous attack or defense, good grappling, or energetic holding all refer to a dog's fine bite ability.

  In the KNPV testing regulations for Police Dog 1, we can also see what is considered to be excellent dog behavior:

- While awaiting the commands for the exercises, the dog remains next to the handler, and she may wait jumping, standing, sitting, or lying down.

  Ideal handler behavior is also listed:

- Since the actions of the handler must be regarded as affecting the work of the dog, the handler must ensure a peaceful appearance that shows confidence.

- Commands should be brief and clear and should not be given in an excessively loud manner. It is up to the handler to decide what words to use. Commands must, however, be related to the exercise to be performed. No corrections are allowed.

- A whistle may only be used for calling the dog, and when performing exercise M of Part 3, Recall of the Pursuing Dog.

- The handler holds his or her hands no higher than waist height when coming and going, and during the exercises while the handler is in motion.

- Throughout the testing and the execution of the exercises, the dog in no way may be held, except for when working on the Heeling on Leash exercise.

- The handler must leash and unleash the dog at the place the judge has appointed. This place is chosen in such a way that handler and dog in both situations must show about 82 feet (25 m) of general obedience.

- Throughout the test, except in the exercise Heeling on Leash, the collar and leash may not be visible to the dog.

- During the test, no compulsion, choke or pinch collars, or groin lines may be used. Use of electronic appliances by which dogs can be corrected, whether or not at a distance, is not permitted. Use of such equipment results in immediate exclusion of handler and dog from the test.

- While presenting and performing the exercises, the handler does not give food rewards to the dog.

16

Decoy and Dog

To protect his body from bites and scratches, decoys must always wear proper protection clothes. These include bite pants, jacket and bite sleeve, a leather apron and bite sleeve, or a full-body bite-protection suit. Decoys must also wear proper footwear that will allow them to gain purchase on the soft ground of a training field, as well as on a hard surface.

Clothing and Injuries

If a decoy wears the wrong protection clothes, or if his gear is old and worn out, both decoy and dog may become injured. For example, a frayed bite sleeve can quickly lead to tooth injuries. The fraying threads on the sleeve can wrap around or go between the dog's teeth and cause damage to teeth and gums, or even ruin teeth. Also, a sleeve that is too hard can lead to injuries such as broken teeth and damage to the tooth enamel. Therefore, the barrel of the bite sleeve should be compressible, and the sleeve cover should be well-fitted to the barrel, not too tight, but not too loose either. Frayed sleeve covers should be replaced immediately. Buckles on sleeves (fortunately we rarely see these) and pants or jackets must be protected so the dog cannot become hooked on them.

To protect his body from bites and scratches, the decoy must always wear protection gear. This drawing shows the protection suit for Schutzhund (IPO). On the photos in this chapter, we can see the bite suit of the Dutch police dog organization, KNPV.

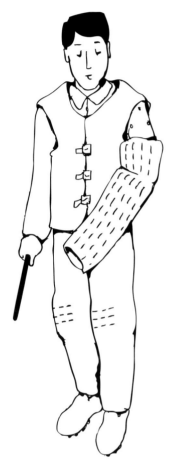

Poor technique on the part of the decoy can also lead to injuries in dogs. Neck and sternum injuries can result from improper catching (such as blocking) and back or internal organ injuries can follow misplaced hits with the stick. Neck and sternum injuries, unfortunately, are not infrequent for dogs undergoing this training. To prevent this, decoys must undergo proper training before working with dogs.

Unfortunately, decoys also sustain injuries in their work with dogs. Several of these injuries can be easily prevented. At so many

When trained correctly, a protection dog is not only muscular and fit but also properly behaved.

training fields we see decoys making the same mistakes over and over again:

- before starting work, no warm up;
- after bite work, no cooling down; as well as
- improper clothing, poor footwear, and poor technique.

For both dogs and decoys, bite work constitutes a top sport that is impossible to engage in without proper training and preparation. A good decoy, therefore, ensures he engages in interval training (protection work is an explosive sport) and makes sure he has muscular strength (back, arms, and legs); balance (judo exercises help); and endurance (after all, he must treat the last dog the same as the first in a training session).

Warm-up and Cool-down for the Decoy

There is no doubt that time spent warming up and cooling down will improve a decoy's level of performance and accelerate the recovery process needed before and after bite work training or competition. Decoys should, therefore, incorporate warm-up and cool-down activities into training and competition routines. The warm-up prepares the body for activity even as it helps prevent injuries to muscles, which are more susceptible to injury when cold. The cool-down helps the body clear lactic acid that builds up in muscles during activity. Less lactic acid means less soreness and stiffness the next day.

The ideal decoy warm-up depends on the number of dogs the decoy has to train, their level of training, and the age and condition of the decoy. The intensity of the warm-up should begin at a low level and gradually build to the level of intensity required during bite work training. For most decoys, five to 10 minutes is enough. However, in cold weather the duration of the warm-up should be increased. The warm-up prepares the body and mind for the bite work, and it increases the body's core temperature, heart rate, and breathing rate.

At minimum, the warm-up should consist of the following:

- jogging to increase body temperature;
- active stretching exercises to reduce muscle stiffness: joint rotations, neck mobility exercises, shoulder circles, arm swings, side bends, hip circles and twists, squats, leg swings, and lunges; and
- some easy runs over 98 to 164 feet (30–50 meters), focusing on correct running technique.

With a warm-up like this in place, the decoy will experience:

- increased speed of contraction and relaxation of warmed muscles;
- reduced muscle stiffness because of the dynamic exercises;
- greater economy of movement because of lowered viscous resistance within warmed muscles;
- greater oxygen utilization by warmed muscles because hemoglobin releases oxygen more readily at higher muscle temperatures;
- better nerve transmission and muscle metabolism, again because of higher muscle temperatures (a specific warm-up can facilitate the motor unit recruitment required for all movements that have to be performed in the heavy decoy work);

- increased blood flow through active tissues as local vascular beds dilate, increasing metabolism and muscle temperatures;
- higher heart rate to start; and
- improved mental focus on the bite work.

Too many decoys neglect the cool-down at the end of a training session, too. It is just as important as the warm-up, especially after vigorous bite work, because the body needs time to slow down and the cool-down provides an important step in recovery. The cool-down should occur immediately after the bite work activities and should last between five and 10 minutes. The cool-down can include the same sort of exercises as the warm-up, but with low-intensity body movements, such as jogging or walking substituted for running. Stretching after activity also helps to ensure maximum flexibility, relaxes the muscles, and returns them to their resting length.

A decoy cool-down should consist of the following components:

- walking to decrease body temperature and remove waste products from the working muscles; and
- static stretching exercises because they help muscles relax, and they realign muscle fibers and re-establish their normal range of movement (stretches should be held for approximately 10 seconds each).

The benefits of an appropriate cool-down are as follows:

- increased dissipation of waste products, including lactic acid;
- reduced potential for delayed onset of muscle soreness (DOMS) that occurs some 24 to 48 hours after intense exercise, usually involving eccentric contractions. (DOMS causes increases in intracellular pressure that irritates the nerve endings, producing swelling and local pain. The soreness can be an indication of potential muscle adaptation to follow, but if it persists or is debilitating, it could indicate overtraining or damage to large muscular tissue.);
- reduced chances of dizziness or fainting caused by the pooling of venous blood at the extremities;

- reduced level of adrenaline in the blood; and
- a more efficient return of the heart rate to its resting rate.

Both warm-up and cool-down should include stretching activities. Active stretches move the muscle groups through the full range of movement required in the activity being performed (hence the name: active stretching). Static stretching is appropriate during the cool-down and can be used to improve flexibility. Some rules decoys should follow when stretching appear below:

1. Warm up the body before stretching.
2. Stretch before and after decoy work (active stretching during the warm-up, static stretching during the cool down).
3. Stretch all muscle groups involved in the decoy work.
4. Stretch gently and slowly: never bounce or stretch rapidly.
5. Stretch gently to the point of mild discomfort, never pain.
6. Do not hold your breath when stretching; breathing should be slow and easy.
7. Never make stretches competitive.

Decoys and dogs should both engage in warm-up and cool-down activities when training and entering competitions/trials.

Warm-up and Cool-down for the Dog

In protection work, dogs experience strain on the mouth (teeth), neck (cervical vertebrae), and back (dorsal vertebrae and spinal column). To prepare the dog's body for this work, warm-up exercises are strongly recommended. Like people, dogs need to warm up to avoid injuries. It is always wise to warm up, especially for the sake of muscles, but also for the ligaments, tendons, and joints. Besides, a warm-up reduces the possibility of chronic symptoms and injuries, because the dog's body is much better able to handle the physical load of the protection training when her body is warmed up and ready to go. The cool-down is also important for dogs as it helps them recover from the activity of training.

THE PROTECTION DOG WARM-UP

By doing warm-up exercises, the dog's body will be prepared for the work it has to do. A dog that begins without a warm-up (so, cold) starts her duty in training or operational service as a protection dog with muscles, ligaments, and joints that are insufficiently supplied with blood. The blood has to transport the energy and oxygen to the muscles and, after energy consumption, drain off the waste products from those muscles.

All muscles hold some glycogen as a small energy source for emergency energy requirements. This can be drawn on without oxygen, so even without a warm-up, muscles can always function. This glycogen is enough for, at the most, two minutes of performance, which explains why a dog without a warm-up can still, for a short time, go at full speed and put in a great effort.

The disadvantages of using this energy source without enough oxygen is the production of lactic acid (lactate) and a minor energy yield as a consequence of an inefficient (oxygen-free) combustion of glycogen. If there is enough oxygen in the blood, glycogen produces eight times more energy, and no lactate builds up.

In the past it was thought that the build-up of lactic acid caused muscular pain, but that is not true. Aching muscles are caused by a lot of small injuries (small ruptures) in the muscular tissue. Nevertheless, lactate has a negative effect on muscles. Its presence causes muscle fibers to hold fluid and swell. Therefore, the circulation of blood decreases, and because of that oxygen delivery decreases.

A good warm-up followed by activity translates to less glycogen energy used, less lactic acid formed, and lactate (like other waste products) drained away faster than if there were no warm-up. Furthermore, better circulation helps not only the muscles but also the tendons and ligaments, which, when warm, resist more stretching, which means the possibility of ruptures of these tissues decreases (a load will not soon be an overload). Warm tendons and ligaments are especially important for dogs about to engage in the exercises; the biggest danger to "cold" dogs comes by way of injuries to these tissues.

The warm-up also has a good effect on the joints. Regular, unweighted movements of the joints during the warm-up result in the production of more synovial fluid, which ensures lubrication and maintenance of the cartilage of the joints both during and after a performance. A safe warm-up for the dog consists of three phases.

PHASE 1: RELAXED START-UP OF THE BODY (TWO MINUTES)
In this phase, the muscles, heart, and vascular system are slowly activated from a resting state. A good, relaxed start-up might be calmly walking with your dog, and after one minute moving into an easy trot.

PHASE 2: INCREASING THE CIRCULATION (THREE TO SIX MINUTES)
The trot at the end of Phase 1 is also the start of Phase 2. Increase the tempo of the easy trot over two or three minutes to a full trot. Trot forward along a straight line, but also in circles, ensuring that the muscles that permit sideward movements are also activated and supplied with blood. You can use a bike for this phase, or simply run alongside your dog.

PHASE 3: STRONG MUSCULAR EXERTION AND ACTIVE STRETCHING
(ONE TO TWO MINUTES)

In Phase 3, you make sure your dog's muscles contract violently and undergo active stretching so she will be fully prepared for the bite work ahead. We advise you to do this by trotting up and down a hill or slope. The advantage of a hill or slope is that the dog also actively stretches: uphill the hindquarters; downhill the forequarters.

As an alternative in this phase, your dog can also sprint, but ideally not at full speed, so not after a thrown ball. Therefore exercises like the Send Away and the Recall are much better for this phase, although they do not allow for active stretching.

STRETCHING AND OTHER WARM-UP EXERCISES

When humans warm up, we often passively stretch our muscles, which is ideal preparation for endurance sports because the muscular tension decreases and the circulation increases. This is not ideal, however, for dogs in protection training because a lower muscular tension also means slower contracting muscles. But active stretching of the muscles keeps the muscular tension at a high level—so this is the kind of stretching protection dogs need.

There are other exercises that also help warm up the dog, such as the attended handstand, by which we carefully shake loose the hindquarters and the back. It is also possible to teach the dog to make a "let's play bow," by which the dog sags through her forelegs. This is a good exercise for loosening up the muscles. Encouraging your dog to circle around you (holding a treat in hand can help with this) is also a good warm-up exercise because it will help her move smoothly, which in turn helps strengthen the vertebral column.

After the warm-up, you might want to teach your dog some exercises in which she becomes aware of her own body and her separate limbs. For example, let your dog walk through or over a ladder that lies horizontally, about four inches (10 cm) above the ground. This helps her learn to coordinate her hind legs. By walking over beams of different sizes lying at different heights above the ground, your dog can also become more aware of her limbs. Placing beams down at different distances from each other, some of them sloping, then having your dog walk over the course set by those beams, teaches your dog to look where to place her feet. Such exercises help prevent physical injuries and mental problems for protection dogs in operational service in areas with difficult surfaces on which to walk, such as in mountains or wooded areas with lots of trees on the ground.

THE IDEAL PROTECTION DOG COOL-DOWN

The cool-down should help your dog recuperate quickly after her fine performance on the training field or in service. After the intense activity associated with protection work, a dog's muscles have to top up their glycogen stock; small damages in muscles, tendons, and ligaments have to be repaired; and all waste products first have to leave the muscles and then the dog's body. Your dog's muscles will recuperate best if you make sure she cools down after exercising, allowing lactate build-up to reduce to contribute to glycogen stocks.

Cool-downs for humans have three key elements: stretching of the muscles, massage, and an easy run to recover. The first element, stretching of the muscles, is only performed if there are no ruptures in the muscle fibers (aching muscles), and then we stretch until just before the pain barrier. Unfortunately, we cannot ask our dogs if their muscles ache or if they've reached their pain threshold, but we can assume that such ruptures are present, given the high intensity of bite work. But it's impossible to know the pain threshold and therefore the moment at which to stop stretching. So, in view of both risks, it's unwise to facilitate your dog's stretching after training.

Massage could be a good choice if your dog can fully relax her muscles and if you know how to do it. Most of the time, however, this is hardly practical, although dogs do appreciate massage. It has a salutary influence on dogs, and most of them fall asleep during it. What sort of massage to give depends on the state of the muscles. Hard muscles (hypertonic) have to get a soothing massage in order to relax. Flabby muscles (hypotonic) need a stimulating massage.

In the end, however, the most common dog cool-down is an easy run. This is simple to do: after training, trot easily for two or three minutes, then pace for about two minutes; if you do this, most of the muscles, joints, and ligaments will be able to reach the cool-down targets.

Please remember how important it is for dogs to cool down after training. Don't go directly from the training field to the car, or even play fetching drills with balls. Instead, trot and then walk easily for about five minutes. In this manner your dog can recover and be ready to turn in another top performance on the field at the next session.

The Art of Training

Correct training produces well-muscled, aerobically conditioned, and properly behaved protection dogs even as it keeps dogs healthy, happy, and uninjured. The art of training athletic animals resides in avoiding sudden, large step-ups in the workload. Everything should be done by increments. A training program that consists of many small steps will prevent injury but take a longer time to bring a dog to top-record performances. Very large increments, even though they speed up the training period, are a strain on the dog, predisposing her to injury or an unhappy disposition.

The spacing of training sequences is also an important factor. Spaced too far apart, adaptations are partially or totally lost. Too close, however, and the dog cannot cope, again predisposing her to injury or mental problems.

The ideal increments and frequency are obviously interrelated, so handlers and trainers must observe the dogs in their care and decide when the next training session should be according to how they have coped with their last training session. We increase the step-up or increase the frequency if the dog has coped well, but, if she has not, we give the dog a longer rest between workouts and/ or lessen the workload. Older dogs that have been well trained all of their active lives need less training to achieve and maintain their condition than do younger dogs. Too many training sessions may strongly diminish their interest.

Defensive and Prey Drives

We will now explain the difference between training bite work out of defensive drive and bite work out of prey drive, as is done in IPO training. The defensive drive is the dog's willingness to pro- tect herself and threatened pack mates, such as the handler or a member of the family. Out of her defensive drive, a dog will resist the decoy's threats without hesitation and defend herself and her handler. Some dogs have a stronger defensive drive than others. Dogs with a good defensive drive and natural bite can often be recognized when they are only pups. They bite into almost every- thing; they bite your trousers and are definitely not impressed when you try to keep them away from that biting; and if they get hold of something that you want to take from them, they growl and snarl.

As soon as your dog gets hold of an article that the decoy wants to take from her, she will growl and snarl.

Because dogs have been selectively bred for beauty for so many years, these days, even in working dogs, many animals have weak characters, which have diminished or are missing the natural defensive drive. This is also true for many dogs with which one wishes to do bite work; as a result, humans have discovered something to solve the problem. We use the dog's prey drive to stimulate her to perform the bite work. The prey drive is very similar to the hunting drive, and originally the prey drive grew out of the attempt not only to hunt game but also to catch and to kill it to satisfy both the dog's own hunger and that of her young. This drive is also present in many of our pet dogs; however, under the influence of the play drive, it is now often associated with chasing toys. We can employ the dog's prey drive to help us teach her to chase a decoy because that decoy has the "prey": the bite sleeve or the tug. To satisfy her prey drive, she will always "capture" the decoy's sleeve. To stimulate her defensive drive, we also ensure the dog learns that she will always win the fight with the decoy.

Testing the First Bite

The best potential protection dogs are the ones that are not interested in the sleeve as prey but that work from a natural, social aggression, the inborn natural sharpness related to the defensive drive. Training protection work is rather easy with these dogs. Whether a dog has a fine, natural defensive drive or not, however, she has to be taught when she is allowed to bite and when not.

Because the dog's defensive drive has to be stimulated in order for her to bite, you should not start bite work with a young dog. The dog has to be mature, both mentally and physically, to handle this heavy training. You can test a dog's potential bite ability when she is about nine months old. You can start her off by encouraging her to bite a tug, and then graduate to the puppy sleeve, a bite sleeve specially designed for young dogs. Fire her up with your encouraging words, and then ask the decoy to offer her the sleeve to bite. What you will see is your dog's natural bite, which is genetically anchored. If you want to train your dog for protection work, that first bite into the sleeve should be a hard and full bite that does not weaken.

If your dog does not bite in this particular way, protection training with her will be very difficult, if not impossible. Many may disagree and say you can teach a dog how to bite. But if you have to use a lot of tricks to get a young dog to bite the sleeve, someday, at a crucial point in time, that dog will walk away instead of defending you. We must say here, though, that if you are only interested in taking your dog through IPO or other top-sport training as a recreational pursuit, it is possible to try to train a dog that doesn't have a natural bite. This is because the stakes are not as high as they are for protection dogs and their handlers.

Decoy Behavior

For each handler and each organization concerned with bite training, the decoy plays an important role. The decoy must himself be a skillful dog handler who knows how to behave around dogs. All organizations that offer protection exercises on a training field should have or educate a capable decoy; and they should reward and cherish him. A raw decoy can ruin the best genetically predisposed dogs, without the handler even noticing. The decoy has to know the examination regulations, but he must also know how to behave so the exercises always have a value for practice. He must know to adapt his actions to the particular natures of each dog he trains, which is why no rigid training system can be made for decoys.

When in contact with a dog that has never before encountered protection work, the decoy behaves gently. He must avoid anything that might frighten the dog. As the dog gains courage, the decoy must become more energetic in his attacks. If the dog's feeling of superiority and confidence continues, the decoy can carefully

The decoy should be a skillful dog handler who knows how to behave around dogs.

administer touches and hits with the stick, and so the dog gradually becomes "stick-proof."

Initially the decoy does not use a bite tug or a bite pillow, but instead he flips a wet leather bite rag out to the dog. If the dog bites the rag, she will know right away that she must bite down hard, otherwise the decoy will easily pull it out of her mouth. The decoy will judge whether or not the dog's grip is sufficient—if it is, he will allow the dog to take the rag. The next step is for the decoy to employ a bite tug or a bite pillow. With this tool, held down so the dog can easily grip it and win the short fight, the decoy can help instill a feeling of confidence in the dog, even as he increases her belligerence.

If the dog is a confident biter and shows defensiveness against the tug, the decoy can begin working with her in a bite suit—or wearing protective pants, jacket, and bite sleeve—but in a way that does not draw attention, so that the dog does not notice the change in attire. If the dog bites well after an attack, the decoy will stop his action. Soon, the dog will herself realize that her defensive behavior was sufficient and will stop biting. Note that a dog must never attack a quietly standing decoy. Improperly trained dogs sometimes nip at unmoving decoys or nip them during the Transport exercise.

A good decoy knows that he should not immediately employ the stick on a beginning dog that executes a powerful bite. Good decoys also do not uproot dogs' teeth by violently jerking the sleeve or tug while the dog is biting.

We have several times seen very bad decoy work, and we have also found clever dogs that reject working with decoys wearing bite suits because they remind them of bad decoys. Other dogs have recognized the purposelessness of their attacks on the agitators in protective suits. We have known dogs that were excellent in protection work practice and yet would not see the decoys in their protective suits as real threats.

On the other side of this issue, you must work to prevent your dog from assuming that the attacks of suited-up decoys on the training field are the only ones she must ward off. To do this, ensure she works (muzzled, of course) with an unprotected decoy in other places, such as at home and especially at night. If you train your dog this way, she will do well during tests and also will stand her ground in the real world.

In the end, if you want a good protection dog, you need a good decoy and skilled helpers. Successful handlers and dogs owe their success to fine decoys.

Dog Behavior

A protection dog should have a steadiness of temperament, but she should also be combative (courageous, bold, or possessing the fighting instinct) and hard. Without these qualities, especially the former, as a rule we can't expect true guardian instincts. Of course, dogs that show little or no fighting instinct are not necessarily cowards. These dogs may have been raised badly. If you want to train a dog for protection work, you should awaken her desire to take and hold early as possible by playing fighting games.

To this end, dog owners are best served by a rolled-up jute bite tug or a long bite tug with two handles. With this tug, you can irritate your dog with all sorts of movements, encouraging her to grasp and bite. If the young dog bites well, walk backward to let her feel the resistance on the tug, and then slowly relax the resistance so the dog feels she is the stronger one in the fight. This is a kind of tug of war that you control, allowing the dog to win even as she learns to firmly grip the tug.

TEACHING THE OUT

On the whole, the young dog's behavior—from her powerful urge to fight to her angry sounds to the hard shine in her eyes—should show us that she is pleased with the fighting games. At this point, you can try to teach her the Out. The moment the dog opens her mouth to get a better grip, immediately pull the tug away, stand up straight, and keep the tug high. With the retraction we clearly give the command "Out." Pull the tug away, and in this manner, stop the game before your dog decides she is tired of it and "outs" the tug all by herself. Once your dog is accustomed to the Out, you can try to do this without a command and by suddenly standing still, just like a decoy who shows no resistance.

After some time, introduce other people to the fighting game. These people play with your dog according to the rules mentioned, but you are the only one to give the "Out" command.

FIGHT THE MAN, NOT THE SLEEVE

Through improper protection dog training, a dog can come to the opinion that the sleeve or tug is the only thing she should bite. We have seen dogs in tests or demonstrations that stay with the sleeve and are not interested in the decoy. In such cases, an error in training has occurred. To ensure the dog understands that she should apply her energy not to the sleeve but to the attacking or fleeing man, the decoy should drop the tug or sleeve to the ground after the training exercises are over. If the dog (initially held on a leash) continues to fight with the dropped sleeve, the unprotected decoy should use his stick to threaten the dog. This will teach her that all danger comes from the man, not the sleeve.

INTRODUCING THE STICK

If your dog is doing well in the training thus far, as you play the fighting game you can also begin to use the tug—not a stick—to administer some gentle touches on her back. From there, graduate to using the stick. You will already have a sense of your dog's disposition and will know how far you can go with this. If she shows timidity or reticence, immediately stop and, before using the stick again, try to increase her courage and hardness by continuing with the fighting game.

OTHER METHODS OF TRAINING

Protection work and biting can also be trained with another proven method. Use a chain or rope to tether your dog in a quiet, somewhat-secluded place, and give her a piece of your clothing to lie down on. Go away a short distance, so that you can still see her but she cannot see or smell you. Your dog will become restless and look around to find you. At this point, send an unconfident-looking stranger (a decoy) in protection gear toward the dog. This person should circle around the dog, moving in and out, making hits and sorties. Every dog—even those with little courage—will be aroused by this behavior.

Come toward your dog and say, "Watch him," then loosen the chain or rope and send the dog out with "Get him!" Now the decoy has to flee and at the same time give your dog the opportunity to bite the sleeve or another place on the bite suit. Your dog must feel that she is the winner after this altercation. Repeat this exercise often, varying it, perhaps, with the decoy attacking you, the handler.

DIFFICULTY BITING

Some dogs have difficulty biting because of incorrect treatment: they feel they are not allowed to bite. In this case, the decoy encourages the dog by hitting her lightly with a loosely held jute tug or with a French linen bite pillow. The decoy can also encourage the dog with the wet leather rag, leaving it in the dog's mouth

A dog's bite work is good when it has a generous attack, good grappling, and energetic holding or defense.

and jumping back in "fear." With caution, again showing fear, the decoy then takes the rag away from the dog and repeats this exercise a few times. Later, as the dog becomes emboldened to bite, the decoy (or the handler) will start administering touches with a stick. For dogs that are "stick shy," the decoy will first use a rolled-up newspaper, then a cardboard tube, a piece of a bike tire, a soft stick, and then a thin, rattan stick. At the beginning, always leave the object to the dog, which makes her aware of the feeling of her power and strengthens her courage. It is the urge to possess the handler's property that encourages the dog to defend her handler.

17

Raising for Protection

Protection training offers us two important elements: the dog learns to warn us against danger (watchfulness), and in case of danger learns how to help us to eliminate the threat (defense).

A watchful dog not only barks when a stranger approaches her owner's property. She also must learn (from her handler) to report the presence of other people when out in a terrain that is strange to her, such as wooded areas, gardens, or buildings. To train a dog for this purpose, we first have to teach her to bark on command. Furthermore, the dog has to show that not every human is her friend, not even when people offer her a snack such as sausages or dog biscuits.

There are four important exercises for raising a protection dog from a puppy:

- Bark on Command and Be Silent,
- Distrusting Strangers,
- Refusing Food, and
- Bite Work and Out.

To prepare the young dog for her future tasks as a protection dog, we have developed an excellent working method. As with everything we write about, we have practiced our method for many years. We developed this method for raising young dogs to become protection dogs because we realized that many modern-day dogs lack courage, but they normally show enough drive for biting (sharpness). However, because of the apparent fearlessness of their dogs, many dog owners are bamboozled. They do not know the difference between courage and sharpness.

Courage is fearlessness and inevitably shows itself when a dog is attacked by a human, even when the handler is not present or if the dog is in strange surroundings. Bite work on the training field will not tell us if dogs have courage, but how a dog bites will show how sharp she is. The handler is always in the vicinity on the training field, so most dogs in that environment show no lack of apparent courage. A lot of dogs, however, will demonstrate a completely different temperament when the handler is not present and the decoy threatens them. In this situation, dogs that only have the "bite drive" run away in fear.

The exercise Bite and Out is a type of fighting game between handler and dog. The decoy doesn't figure in this exercise, since most of the time a stranger frightens a young dog. The young dog should not become fearful, because if she has a lack of courage, this would be visible in the fight with the strange decoy, and that has to be avoided.

This fighting game demands that the handler have the necessary willpower to push the dog to act. There is hardly another exercise that demands so much of the handler in terms of being able to understand the dog's character. Everyone who works with dogs for as long a time as this exercise requires will experience this. The exercise is built up in such a way that you don't need to worry about your dog relapsing. We and many others have trained our dogs this way for many years, and we have had excellent results, particularly with dogs that aren't terribly courageous. This method is also very good for dogs that lack sharpness. Dogs that have no lack of courage or sharpness learn to control their spirit with these exercises.

Barking

To begin to teach your dog to bark on command, you must first find something that stimulates your dog to bark. When such a prickle has been found, then with every bark you should give a command such as "Bark," "Loud," or "Search." If your dog barks more, reward her: "Good girl, bark!" In the beginning, the dog can get her reward after barking two or three times; later on, let her bark a while longer before rewarding her. With dogs that don't bark easily, the exercises must not be repeated too often, because then they really won't want to bark.

To figure out what gets your dog barking, you have to be imaginative. Following are some possibilities to try with your dog.

- Fill your dog's food bowl and hold it high enough that she can smell it but cannot reach it. Her impatience may inspire her to bark.

- Tether your dog somewhere and then play with a strange dog hanging around nearby, or pet that dog. Her jealousy may make her bark.

- If your dog knows the routine that happens before going for a walk, perform this routine and then put your dog on a tether or in the kennel instead. That will get a lot of dogs to bark.

- Tether your dog somewhere outside and walk away from her. This is also likely to get her to bark. As soon as your dog begins to bark, say "Bark, good girl, bark," pet her and go away again. This can be repeated three to four times. After a break, repeat the exercise.

Your dog can also be brought to barking by sounds. A dog we knew that was not willing to bark suddenly barked nonstop when guitar strings were touched while the handler was dusting, for example. This prickle also worked later on, and guitar strings thus became the tool that taught the dog to bark.

For as long as the dog doesn't bark on command, the same prickle that caused the barking must be used to encourage barking. From the beginning, the command for barking can be accompanied by a discreet signal (of the hand or the head). For instance, in the dog's view, while giving the command to bark, tap your forefinger and thumb of the same hand together. That way the dog will combine the command and the signal, and later on she will react to the signal alone with loud barking.

When she receives the command "Get him," your dog must hold the person indicated in his place under all circumstances.

Correct timing isn't always easy for dogs.

Be Silent

A dog that barks on command must also learn to be silent on command. As with barking, you can teach silence to a young dog as well as an older one. This exercise does not demand physical effort, so we can start as early as possible without any problem. Besides, a dog that is longer in training will be more alert and excited by things happening in her vicinity. She will often react to her surroundings by barking. Before this becomes a habit, we must teach her to control herself.

When you begin teaching this exercise, start in a relaxed way at home. While your dog is lying down in her place, sit beside her. Ask a helper, invisible to the dog, to make strange sounds, ring the doorbell, or knock at the door. Give a soft whispering command "Quiet" or "Silent," and if necessary hold her mouth shut at the same time.

When your dog understands what is expected of her, go outside, go into some shrubbery with the dog, and again have a helper make a lot of noise or strange sounds. Or, have a helper command another dog to bark at a distance, and at a later stage someone can fire a shot from far away. At first, have this noisy helper at some distance from the dog. Throughout all of these trials, stay close to your dog and give her the command; ensure she doesn't make a sound. Your attitude and way of speaking, in an excited whispering tone, will make it clear to your dog what is expected. As with barking on command, you can combine a discreet hand signal with the command to be silent.

If your dog shows that she can control herself, the distance at which the noise is made can be gradually reduced. The final requirement for this exercise has your sitting or lying dog staying in place without barking or making sounds, not reacting to sounds or things happening around her.

Distrusting and Refusing Food

Dogs that are suspicious of strangers in their youth, or that show their teeth, bark, or bristle their back hair when a stranger is enticing, do so out of fear; they carry the germ of cowardice in them. It is a lot better when a young dog is friendly with strangers and goes to them when enticed. This confidence is a lot easier to change than it is to make a suspicious dog into a courageous protection dog.

A dog can be cured of his confidence with strangers, if desired, by two influences: that of the stranger and that of the handler. A stranger entices the dog; if the dog responds, she gets a light tap on the snout from the stranger. If the dog turns back disappointed, then the handler calls her and praises her. The dog learns that only her owner treats her lovingly, not strangers. The dog's treatment by the stranger should not leave her feeling fearful; that's why the taps have to be as soft as possible. Repeat the enticement regularly with other strangers and, if necessary, children.

After training this way for some time, if your dog doesn't react to being enticed by strangers, you can ask a "stranger" to tempt her with pieces of meat. A helper takes a good-sized piece of meat in his or her left hand and shows it to the dog. At the moment the dog wants to take the meat, the helper quickly gives her a tap on the snout with his or her free hand. When the dog no longer finds this tempting, the helper throws the meat in the direction of the dog. Now you have to ensure that your dog doesn't take the meat. As soon as she comes close to the food, issue a powerful "No!" and even chase your dog away from the meat. This has to be trained regularly, although skipping a few weeks every now and then is okay. Every time you train this exercise, your dog must be tempted by different people, at different times and places, and by different food.

To teach a dog to refuse food as correctly as possible, which can be very difficult for some dogs, do not allow other members of the family or visitors to feed the dog out of their hands, and never allow her to pick up food from the ground. Only you—nobody else—may hand-feed a reward to your dog.

With dogs that already distrust strangers, we train the refusing of food in another way. The stranger doesn't use the food to entice

A helper takes a chunk of meat in his hand and shows it to the dog.

the dog to come, so the dog's fear won't be aroused. The stranger quietly throws the food to your dog. If she shows interest in the thrown meat, call out a sharp "No!" Don't chase her away from the meat, but go to her quietly and take her away by the collar. Distrustful dogs have to be trained to refuse food less often than dogs with more confidence in strangers.

Bite Work and Out

The "fighting game" between handler and dog we mention at the beginning of this chapter is a fantastic exercise. Its value cannot be overestimated for a reliable protection dog: as a result of this game, the dog is prepared for anything. Through the game she also becomes accustomed to the absolutely necessary obedience required of protection dogs. The exercise also has the benefit of making handler and dog an unbreakable team and gives the dog healthy exercise that stimulates the development of her muscles.

The article needed for this exercise is a rolled-up burlap sack or a puppy tug. A burlap feed sack can be cut open and rolled on its length. Tie one of the ends with a rope, then knot the sack up a few times along its 28-inch (70-cm) length, but do not tie up the last eight inches (20 cm).

When your tool is ready, hold it at the closed end and move it back and forth in front of your dog and pull it over the ground. With "Get him," encourage your dog to catch the burlap roll. Keep it up until the dog catches and bites it. Once she catches the sack, ensure she holds it in her mouth. To do that, as soon as your dog bites in, pull the roll so your dog feels resistance equal to her own against the roll. The dog has to feel resistance or she will release the roll on her own soon after biting in.

You cannot let your dog know that you are stronger than she is. You may only offer as much resistance as that used by your dog. If she pulls at the roll, you, too, should pull. Draw it back, then pay it out again, and each time she pulls, say, "Good girl, get him."

If your dog has hung on to the roll for some minutes, pull the roll quietly toward you, with your dog hanging from it. Reaching under her chin, place your forefinger and thumb behind the canines of her lower jaw, the forefinger a bit farther out onto the tongue, and this will make your dog open her mouth directly. When her mouth is open, pull the roll out of her mouth and say, "Out." The burlap roll now has to be held in such a way that your dog cannot immediately bite it again.

Depending on your dog's level of interest in this fighting game, you can carefully begin to teach her the three important commands: "Watch him," "Get him," and "Out." The command "Watch him" has to prepare the dog for the coming fight but does not encourage her to fight. The command to fight is "Get him." In many countries, however, where it is against the law to set your dog on people, we recommend that you use another command for bite work, such as "Defend" or "Go ahead." For the dog, however, it doesn't matter what the word combination is—all of the possibilities mean that she is to bite a human, so in the end, teaching any command to fight represents the same violation.

In times of danger, the protection dog helps eliminate threats.

A protection dog is expected to defend her handler directly on command. But to teach her this, she first must clearly learn defense. Defense means fight; so, we first have to teach her to fight, and for this we use a certain command. We must never fashion our dogs into fighting machines that are so sharp and biting that nobody can get near them. Such dogs can absolutely never be used as protection dogs. A dog must not only learn to bite, she must also learn when not to bite.

To teach the dog not to bite, you must carefully train her to understand the "Out" command. We want courageous protection dogs that defend us to the hilt, if necessary. But we also want protection dogs that immediately obey the softest command.

The Three Commands

We can train a reliable protection dog through bite work if the dog learns three important commands:

1. At the command to be attentive ("Watch him"), nobody is allowed to touch or try to touch the handler or dog anymore.

2. At the command to defend ("Get him"), the dog must keep the person indicated in place by any means.

3. At the command for safety ("Out"), the dog is under no circumstances allowed to bite, or when she is biting (after the command "Get him"), she must immediately release.

In normal situations, it must be possible to shake hands with the decoy, pat him or her on the back, all things that happen regularly in everyday life. But if you have a sharp dog that doesn't respond to "Out," unpleasant things can easily happen.

Train your dog to respond to these commands through the fighting game as follows. Show your dog the burlap roll in such a way that she cannot bite it. In a quiet tone, say, "Watch him," and touch her lightly with the roll. Then hit the ground with the roll and encourage her to "Get him," to catch the roll. If she bites the roll, praise her with "Good girl, get him," and tug at the roll with a force equal to hers. After about one minute, command your dog to "Out" briefly and sharply. When she releases the sack, don't hold it high, but keep it within her reach. However, keep your dog from biting again with your free hand and the warning command "Out." If she tries to bite the roll in spite of that, give her a tap on the snout together with the sharp command "Out." Do NOT punish her by saying "No."

Your dog's character also informs how you should train these commands. With dogs that are sharp, train biting briefly but the Out longer. Let such dogs pull the burlap roll for a short amount of time, but lengthen the sequence after the Out. Put more emphasis on suppressing than on promoting the bite drive.

We handle dogs that are hesitant to bite differently. We let them pull the roll more often and longer, and we train the Out less often and more briefly. If such a dog re-bites after the Out, we let that quietly happen. When the dog becomes less hesitant, and the drive to bite comes to the fore, we change the training pattern to match the one used with dogs that do bite.

The dog also has to slowly get used to soft hits with the burlap roll or the tug. The first time you touch your dog carefully with the roll, move it so it comes at her from below, where she can see it. The fighting game starts as usual with "Watch him." Then you wave the roll quickly in front of your dog and command "Get him." As you do this, let the roll gently come up from your dog's lower right toward the shoulder and neck, so she can catch it very easily. In the beginning, you have to ensure that she can catch the roll right after you touch her with it. But the roll must not be held in front of her snout, because in that position, she will not be as able to catch it. She has to be enticed to grasp the rushing and jumping roll all by herself.

As the training sessions progress, how hard you touch her with the roll increases and varies in terms of what direction the roll is coming from: below, above, the side. When you move the roll down from above to touch your dog with it, make sure it is coming at her from high up, as if you want to give your dog a hard hit, but hit only as hard as your dog can bear. As well, often give the ground beside your dog a hard hit. She must lose all fear of such hits.

The age, physical development, and sensitivity of your dog are important factors to keep in mind when you are deciding how hard you should bring the roll down. The hits should gradually get a bit harder. Make sure you touch your dog on the thighs, against the cheeks, and along the length of her back. Hits on the head or diagonally over the back are not allowed. Only let her bite the roll after your dog has experienced a few hits. The exercise works out as follows.

Hold the burlap roll quietly while commanding, "Watch him." Then, with a sudden movement, swing the roll in such a way that you partially hit your dog as well as the ground beside her. Then command, "Get him," and she is allowed to bite in. Of course, then she is a "Good girl, get him." After a short or long fight, say, "Out." When you have the roll in hand, first quietly hold it before your dog, then softly wave it in front of her, repeating the command "Out" a few times. Your dog is not allowed to bite in now, and you must prevent biting even as you keep the roll within her reach.

Only adult dogs should be asked to jump over ditches. For safety reasons, in the KNPV program, the sides of the ditch must be oblique.

If your dog is working this out correctly, take the roll in your left hand and walk away quietly. She will follow her beloved play article on her own, but she is not allowed to catch it. This exercise lays the foundation for the Transport of the Suspect exercise.

To teach your dog to release well, after the Out, wave the roll in front of her, whip it through the air, turn it in a circle over her head, and at last pet her back quietly with it. With this, the raising of the young dog for protection work can be considered done; further training, as described in the next chapters, will make her a reliable protection dog.

18

Basic Exercises for Protection

In the last chapter, we discussed how to raise a puppy to become a protection dog. In the next chapter, we discuss protection work training for adult dogs. Young or old, a reliable protection dog must first, however, master the two basic exercises discussed in this chapter: Barking on Command and Refusing Offered and Thrown Food.

Barking on Command

Barking is a strong method of communication for dogs, especially if they wish to convey something to humans. If we teach our dogs to make themselves known in several circumstances by barking, we will understand one another better. A protection dog must be able to warn us of certain dangers by barking. Some people define the Barking on Command exercise as an obedience exercise, but in reality it isn't. Obedience exercises demonstrate that the handler has control of his or her dog. If a dog barks on command, she is, of course obedient, but the watchful dog that knows to bark on command is also expected to bark on her own.

In our training method, the dog learns to bark in different positions: sitting, lying down, standing, and in motion. Because a protection dog has to bark at suspicious persons and articles, she should also be taught to bark when she is far away from her handler. We have already described how to teach a dog to bark on command (see Chapter 17). The exercises described there can also be worked out with older dogs.

In this chapter, we want to describe another way to teach dogs to bark at strangers that are threatening her or her handler, a way that also works with older dogs. Tether your dog and ask a "stranger" to threaten her from a distance. In the beginning, stand beside the helper and, with every bark of the dog, say, "Bark, good girl, bark." After a short period, the helper steps back, and you praise your dog, after which the exercise can be repeated. The dog's position, sitting or standing, is unimportant. This time, stand in front of the helper. The latter only threatens with his or her arms when your dog doesn't bark on command. If your dog reacts well, the helper gradually steps back. When she stops barking, try to encourage your dog to bark again, using the same threats the helper was using. In the beginning, be satisfied with a few barks, but later on, allow your dog bark longer, between 15 and 20 times. Gradually pull away the supports to this exercise until your dog barks continuously upon the issue of one command.

By barking, your dog can warn you of danger. This dog barks while guarding a decoy.

At this point, you can take your dog on leash, walk with her, and stop, so she sits down right away. Step in front of her and immediately give the command "Bark." This can be repeated three or four times. It is unimportant if the dog stays sitting, because this exercise is only meant to teach the dog Barking on Command. Once she consistently barks on command, you can worry about the dog's position. For barking on command in the Sit position, let your dog sit and give the command "Bark." If she tries to stand, correct her with "Sit" and "Bark." With this exercise, you first stand in front of your dog, but if all goes well, you can stand more to the side of your dog. Never forget to reward your dog after the exercise.

Barking on Command in motion can easily be taught out of the Sit position, while you stand in front of your dog. If she barks on command in the Sit, slowly step backward and encourage your dog to come and continue barking. If your barking dog follows you, slowly turn, so that she is in the Heel position.

At this point you can also start training the bark in the Stand position by giving the dog the command "Stand" and "Stay," and if necessary also the command "Bark." Begin training for Barking on Command in the Down position with the dog on leash. The dog hears the command "Down," then you put your foot on her leash and give the command "Bark."

It is also advisable to teach your dog to bark from a distance. Tether your dog and tell her to "Stay" or "Wait." Walk about 66 feet (10 m) away from her, turn around, and give the by-now well-known command (eventually only the signal with the hand or the head, as described in the previous chapter), to which she should react with loud barking. Later on, you can ask your dog to wait off leash, and increase the distance you walk away from her.

Trained this way, your dog can be taught very easily to bark at certain articles and persons, whether they stand, sit, or lie down.

Refusing Offered or Found Food

A dog that takes food from strangers, or food thrown in her direction, or takes found food from the ground, can never be a trustworthy guard, sentry, police, or protection dog. She may even die from eating deliberately poisoned food. If a dog can be influenced by offered or found food, her reliability for other tasks is suspect.

It isn't always easy to make a dog 100 per cent foolproof in food refusal, in particular when she is without supervision. In spite of that, we must not neglect this absolutely important exercise. This exercise demands a lot of patience, toughness, and willpower, and you may not always reach the goal. Note that we have already pointed out that a dog must never be fed from the hand of strangers or even other members of your family. Only you, the handler, are allowed to give your dog a reward out of the hand—nobody else.

The exercises for food refusal mentioned in the previous chapter can also work with older dogs. During training, your dog has to be tempted to accept or take food. Such temptations can be built into different exercises, especially obedience training, but never with exercises the dog has not yet mastered. You must always know where the food is laid down or where it will be offered. You must always carefully observe to see if your dog pays attention to found food. If she does, then she must be punished with "No." If she shows interest in found food again, take her on leash with a choke-chain collar, bring her to the food and correct her with a sharp jerk on the leash and the word "No." As noted, if a dog picks food up from the ground, she could die, so she has to be punished immediately for this behavior. One way to observe your dog in this exercise and not waste time is to connect a big piece of meat to a thin fishing line equipped with a bell or alarm system. As soon as your dog touches the meat, the bell rings, and you can correct her with a powerful "No."

Teaching a future protection dog to refuse offered or found food may save her life.

When you come to the point where you ask strangers or decoys to offer food to your dog out of their hands, make sure your dog doesn't attack them and that she doesn't walk away from the offered food. The dog that considers everyone who offers food to be an enemy can cause a lot of damage. If a dog walks away from offered food, she may also be easy to send away from an article she is supposed to be guarding. Train your dog to be indifferent to offered or thrown food.

Tether your dog, then have the helper present food to her. The person shouldn't be too obvious about it. If your dog growls or shows her teeth, the helper must give up the attempt to offer the food but should throw it toward her and quietly go away. You must watch from a distance so you can correct your dog immediately, if necessary. If your dog wants to walk away from the offered food, the helper should leave immediately. Never incite your dog against the helper.

19

Training for Protection

In Chapter 17, we discussed how to raise a young dog to be trained as a protection dog. Chapter 18 discussed foundation exercises dogs of any age need to master before beginning the exercises in this chapter. What follows here is the method we use to introduce the bite work training for protection dogs and the exercises of the Dutch KNPV Police Dog program.

Bite and Out

The first thing we demand of a trained protection dog is that she use her teeth only when we want her to; she has to be taught to bite only on our command. Therefore, we first encourage the sharpness—the drive to bite—in the dog, and when that has happened, we have to take care that we only employ that sharpness when we need to. Never ignite a dog's sharpness so much that you cannot control it.

To train a dog in bite work, the decoy must understand his work very well. A decoy has to be skillful, powerful, and courageous, and preferably also a richly experienced dog handler. He has to recognize the character of each dog, even after working with her briefly. The skills of the decoy are especially important with a dog that isn't talented in bite work. Often the desire to bite lies

The first thing we demand
of our protection dogs is
that they bite only on our
command.

dormant in some dogs but can be brought out through the right approach by the decoy, after which such dogs can become the best protection dogs. A poor decoy will either get nothing out of such a dog or will completely upset her.

During the first bite exercises, ensure your dog is wearing a leather collar and hold her on a leash. The decoy will wave the burlap roll or tug back and forth in front of your dog, after which you can encourage her with "Get him" and then loosen the leash to give her the opportunity to bite. The decoy has to catch the dog skillfully so your dog can bite correctly into the roll. Pay out the line and encourage your dog to hold the bite, while the decoy keeps your dog active by quietly moving the roll back and forth. The decoy should pull against the roll with the same force your dog uses to pull. He moves quietly and doesn't make sudden movements but stimulates your dog to hold on. Continue to encourage your dog with "Get him, good girl, get him," while patting her calmly on her shoulder or side. When she has pulled on the roll for a while, the decoy stops his movements and resistance, and you give the command "Out." After a short pause for praise, this exercise can be repeated.

As soon as your dog shows a correct bite drive, you want to give her a certain structure by getting her used to the three commands: "Watch him," "Get him," and "Out." To this end, the decoy walks quietly toward you and your leashed dog. With an outstretched arm, point at the decoy and clearly say, "Watch him." The decoy walks quietly to a spot a couple of feet in front of you and stands still. In the meantime, your dog is not allowed to try to reach the decoy; if she does, administer a powerful jerk on the leash and again the command "Watch him." Don't give the command "Out" because then she may not bite anymore. "Watch him" is the correct command; it prepares your dog for a possible fight with the decoy.

Now the decoy grabs you around your chest or shoulder, and he holds the burlap roll where the dog can catch it. When the decoy attacks, say, "Get him." You have to keep your dog on a very short leash until she has caught the roll. After a brief or longer fight, the decoy stands still and you give the command "Out." As soon as your dog releases the roll, the decoy quietly walks away.

Further training depends on your dog's behavior. If she is inclined to be too sharp, do less bite work. In this case, the decoy will walk toward you and your dog, stay longer in front of you, and then quietly walk away. He can also pass close by you and your dog or walk around the pair of you. You must not give your dog a command to sit at heel. The dog should be left to choose her position beside you. If the decoy passes you or walks around you, your dog is allowed to turn to watch him. Of course, she has to stay beside you. With dogs that are too sharp, attacks on the handler are practiced only every now and then. We work differently with a dog that isn't sharp enough. This dog will be enticed to bite and fight more often.

After a few days' training, if your dog shows a lot of interest in the decoy, the latter should appear in full bite suit. At this point, your dog should still be working on leash. It is correct if she now lunges toward the decoy on the command "Watch him," and barks or growls. She isn't, however, allowed to jump on him or to bite. If she tries, then she will be kept on a short leash and pressed to stay beside you at the command "Watch him."

Once the decoy is working in the complete bite suit (French, Dutch, or trial suit), you don't use the roll or tug anymore. But you and the decoy will still work out the exercises in the same way. The decoy passes you, walks around you, and then walks away. The decoy can arrange to suddenly attack you from behind.

Because your dog has to bite on command under all circumstances, she also has to be taught to bite a motionless decoy on command. This, of course, is against the common rules of dog sports. But a protection dog may encounter a situation in which it is vital that she bite a person who isn't moving away, such as a person who stops to take out a pistol or a knife. Drilling your dog not to bite a motionless person can make her useless as a protection dog.

The decoy stands quietly about 33 feet (10 m) away from you and your dog. Point to the decoy and say, "Watch him" and, after a short time, "Get him." As soon as your dog is biting in, and not earlier, the decoy puts up a fight, and after a short fight, he stops. You can then give the command "Out."

After every exercise, the decoy walks quietly to you to say goodbye. By now, your dog knows the Out very well. So, when the decoy comes over to say goodbye, give your dog the command "Out," and the decoy will walk calmly over to you, shake your hand, and pat you on the back. The decoy, in principle, must even be able to pet your dog quietly, because your dog has to be taught that after the command "Out," there is no reason to bite anymore.

If all dogs that do bite work were trained in the way described above, there would be no "problematic cases." In this method, the handler fully controls his or her dog and doesn't have to be afraid of uncontrolled attacks, even with sharp dogs.

Transport and Escape

Once your dog has defended you from an attack by the decoy, she can learn how to do the Side Transport and the Escape of the Decoy exercises. With the Transport, you walk at the right side of the decoy and your heeling dog walks between you. She can heel, depending on her obedience, off leash or on, or walk free behind the decoy. Just like in obedience training and trials, turns and stops are made, although not abruptly. You must tell the decoy loudly and clearly what he has to do, for instance walk, turn right, about-turn left, and stop. Before the exercise starts, you should arrange with the decoy the timing of the Escape of the Decoy. When the escape occurs, command your dog to "Get him" and, depending on the sharpness of your dog, a short or long fight follows.

After repeating this exercise several times, put your dog on leash and hold it slack. Now a Back Transport takes place. You and your dog follow the decoy at a distance of about five paces. At first, there are no stops or turns. At a prearranged moment, the decoy runs away, but your dog is not immediately allowed to go after him. If she wants to do that, pull powerfully on her leash and command, "Heel." After you command, "Get him," let go of the leash and allow your dog to pursue. At this point, you should stand still and let your dog do her work with the decoy. When the decoy stands still, make sure you immediately command, "Out." The decoy is never allowed to command the dog to release. The decoy does have to freeze before the Out, though, whether by pre-arrangement with you, the handler, or at your order.

After this, the decoy stands about 98 feet (30 m) away from you—farther away later on in training—and then he walks away. Follow him, with your dog on leash. The decoy "suddenly" runs away at a pre-arranged time, but your dog may only pursue him when you have given her the command to do so. Every time your

Offering resistance to a police officer and a well-trained police
dog is absolutely useless, not to mention painful.

dog has to pursue the escaping decoy, draw her attention by pointing at the decoy and saying "Watch him." If you don't include
that command in the exercise, your dog may only hear you saying
"Out," which is a command not to pursue.

Now and then, before your dog catches up with him, the decoy
must fall down on the ground. The dog is not allowed to bite when
she reaches a prone decoy; if necessary, you may need to command
"Out."

Guarding People

The best way to begin the Guarding exercise is with an Escape of
the Decoy. After your dog has bitten, the decoy stands still. You
are at first in the vicinity, so you can command, "Out," and after
your dog has released, "Watch him." Do not say, "Wait," "Sit," or
"Down," because your dog would then not be permitted to leave
her place.

Now it is up to the decoy's skills to keep the dog in his vicinity.
He will stand still for a while, then he will try to escape. When this
happens, immediately command, "Get him." If your dog bites, the
decoy will stand still, followed by your "Out" and a short pause in

While guarding, your dog must be attentive to the decoy.

which the dog guards the decoy while you say, "Watch him, good girl, watch him." If your dog's attention falters for a moment, the decoy will again try to escape, and you will again command, "Get him." After a short or long fight, the decoy stops again, and after your command to "Out," the dog has to guard him. At this point, go over to the decoy and command him to "Step back" and say, "Hands up." When the decoy complies, your dog should not bite.

Now walk behind the decoy and search and disarm him (take the stick or the pistol). After that, step back to your dog, command the decoy to put his arms down, and the exercise can end with a Side or Back Transport without an escape. After the command "Stop," the decoy stands still, and you and your dog walk away in another direction.

If this exercise goes well, have your dog work it out at increasingly greater distances from you. Regardless of how far your dog is from you, the decoy will ensure she stays within his vicinity. As soon as your guarding dog is not attentive anymore, the decoy will attempt an escape. Depending on your dog's character, the decoy can also attack her and try to chase her away. He also has to threaten your dog with his voice.

Refusing Commands of Strangers

You can train your dog to refuse the commands of strangers not only during obedience exercises but also during bite work training, as when guarding. The decoy will try to make your dog give up guarding with commands like "Go to your handler," "Down," "To your place," "Get away," and so on. The decoy can also drop the stick and try to get your dog to retrieve it.

Hold and Bark

A precondition for this exercise is that your dog is able to bark on command, even at a distance from you, her handler. At first, have your dog work out this exercise while on a long line fastened to a leather collar or solid harness. Hold on to this line between where it is fastened to your dog's collar and where you have tied it to a spring or solid rubber tire that is in turn tied to a tree or post. The spring or tire will soften the impact when the dog stretches to the end of the line. In this exercise, the decoy (without protection gear) stands so far in front of you and your dog that your dog can't reach him. In one hand, he holds the burlap roll, and in the other hand, he holds a finger-thick rattan stick or a soft stick. When you are ready, point at the decoy, command, "Search," and slip the line through your hands as your dog advances toward the decoy until she is about three feet (1 m) in front of him. Then command, "Bark." To ensure your dog better understands the command "Search," give the command in combination with "Bark," so: "Bark, search, bark, search." At first, the decoy can help encourage your dog to bark by making kicking movements or threatening with the stick. Make sure you hold your dog back so she cannot bite.

This dog shows an energetic version of the Hold and Bark.

After she barks for some time, walk quietly over to your dog and praise her exuberantly. Command the decoy to leave, and when the decoy is out of sight, go with your dog back to the starting point. After a while, the decoy will return, and the exercise is repeated. If your dog doesn't attempt to bite, and if she is barking very well, you can try training this exercise without a line. When your dog is off the line, the decoy should be in full protection garb, and he should stand in front of a wall to cover his back. This way, your dog can only bark in front of him.

In a subsequent exercise, your dog doesn't know where the decoy is. After the command "Search," the dog has to *revier*, or search for the decoy and bark if she finds him, but she is not allowed to bite. Most of the time, we use blinds on the training field as hiding places for the decoy, but the protection dog's training should avoid set patterns, so you must train in all possible—even unlikely— places. If everything is going well, the exercises mentioned earlier in this chapter (Transport, Escape, Bite, and Out) can be combined with the exercise Hold and Bark.

Gunfire

Normally, older animals offered for protection dog training are tested on their sensitivity to gunfire before they are allowed to take part in training. The test happens about 82 to 98 feet (25–30 m) away from the handler and the on-leash dog, and the shots are fired within seconds of each other with a .22 starter pistol. Dogs that seem afraid of the shots and try to run or crawl away will, of course, be refused admission to the training. But often dogs that are sensitive or restless in reaction to the noise are also refused. Still, it is possible to get dogs who are a little shot-sensitive (not the ones that are afraid) used to the noise by first firing the shots from a greater distance (328 to 492 feet [100–150 m]). The dog should already have undergone some training and be able to heel correctly on leash. When practicing this gunfire training, always fire when your dog is heeling on leash and never during a stop. The need to focus on the commands of the handler in the heeling exercise will help prevent your dog from responding to the sound of the gunfire. Make sure you correct your dog with a powerful "No" when she lags behind or deviates because of the shot, after which immediately repeat the command for heeling.

Don't try to reassure your dog during the shooting, because this attention just heightens the shot sensitivity. Your job is to help alleviate your dog's propensity to react to the sound of gunfire by focusing her attention on the heelwork; make sure you correct all deviations from correct heeling. Depending on the dog's reactions, the distance between you and where the gun is fired can slowly be decreased.

A young and inexperienced dog may also be sensitive at first to gunfire, perhaps because her handler is nervous, or it's a strange training field with strange persons and other circumstances. So this also has to be taken into account during a sensitivity test. Only when you are calm about everything can you inspire calm and certainty in your dog.

If your dog is shot-sensitive but loves bite work, you can try to help her overcome her sensitivity during bite work training. The decoy, armed with a burlap roll or tug, attacks you, but your dog can't bite because you are holding her on a short leash. The decoy then escapes, and you say, "Watch him." After he has advanced about 98 feet (30 m), send your dog out with the command "Get him." When your dog bites, the decoy catches her correctly on the roll, and a short fight follows, after which the decoy stands still. You have followed your dog to where the fight is. As soon as the decoy is still, ensure your dog releases, and then praise her. Leash your dog. The decoy runs again. Encourage your dog to watch him closely, but continue to hold her back. The decoy continues to walk away, and then he fires a shot when he is about 164 feet (50 m) from you and your dog. Don't give your dog time to be fearful of the gunfire, but instead run with her toward the decoy, shouting a loud "Get him." This way, she will forget her fear and focus her attention in full on the decoy. The dog now may have a nice fight with the decoy. This exercise can be repeated once or twice per training session, but not to the point where your dog gets tired of it.

After one or two weeks of training in this way, allow your dog to wait off leash as you walk in the direction of the decoy, coming to a standstill about 65 feet (20 m) away from him. The decoy fires a shot and attacks you. Encourage your dog to defend you with an intense "Get him, get him." Shortly before the dog reaches the decoy, the decoy lets go of you and catches the dog correctly.

Train consistently so that the shots are gradually fired closer to the dog. You can then vary the training of both the bite work exercises described here. As soon as your dog has lost her fear of gunfire in the exercises, ask someone to fire a gun from a distance when she is biting the decoy. If she releases her grip right after the shot, the decoy should directly attack you, her handler. Encourage your dog to "Get him," and as soon as she has bitten, praise her exuberantly. Dogs that don't react to the shot-test at 49 to 98 feet (15–30 m) can be trained for bite work in the way mentioned on page 207. Ultimately, that exercise will be connected with all the other exercises we write about in this chapter.

The Stick

How insensitive you can make your dog to hits with the stick depends mainly on her innate sensitivity to pain. However, by careful and planned training, we can often improve the dog's insensitivity to pain. The dog got used to hits with the burlap roll or tug during his upbringing and later exercises. The roll causes painless hits, and because of this, any fear of a hit is already nil or negligible.

You can also use a soft, but not too light, leather belt as a second tool to desensitize your dog. It should be at least two inches (5 cm) wide and about 18 inches (45 cm) long. When you use it, only touch the flat of your dog's back. If you use a belt with care, it causes so little pain that it can even be used on sensitive dogs. Even the noise that results when you use a belt doesn't disturb dogs.

The third tool you can use is a long, slender, flexible twig. Hits with this are a bit more painful but will be borne by dogs who have trained with the roll and belt. After that, you can use a rattan stick, and also a rattle baton, a thick bamboo stick split on the underside that makes a rattling sound. If your dog tolerates such sticks, she may be assessed as being confidently tolerant of hits with the stick.

Training dogs not to bite people who are standing still can make them useless as protection dogs.

We want to point out a mistake that very often is made with dogs that bear the hits with the stick very well. Handlers sometimes let decoys hit such dogs more often and harder, mostly to impress other handlers. If the dog later shows a certain degree of disinterest in bite work, the handler doesn't understand why. Most of the time, this disinterest is because of the continuous, excessive hitting the dog has been enduring during bite work.

Hits with a stick should be used seldom during training, and even then for not more than two or three hits at a time. The roll, tug, or belt can be used more often, although some discretion is necessary even with these. When you change from using a gentle tool to a harder one, administer the hits softly at first. If the dog shows sensitivity to a tool, go back to a gentler one. The decoy has to have the skill to place the hits correctly and only when the dog is involved in the fight. He especially has to realize that the dogs he is working with aren't fully trained protection dogs. As well, he must be very careful with shy dogs; when hitting these dogs, the hit should begin high above the dog, but the tool should only slowly come into contact with her.

Sharp dogs that are inclined to display anxiety, as well as dogs that have a lack of sharpness—even when they don't have fear—can be hit before they bite but may not be hit after they have bitten in. After the dog bites in, the decoy just pretends to hit. If they progress in training, they may later receive a few weak hits now and then, as soon as they have bitten in well.

Courage Training

A dog is courageous if she doesn't run from people attacking her and if she will not be chased away, even if the handler isn't nearby. To gradually increase your dog's courage, you can train her in the following way.

The decoy stands 32 feet (10 m) in front of you as you hold your dog by the collar. As the decoy shows your dog threatening movements with the stick, encourage her to be watchful with the words "Watch him." The decoy approaches the dog with arms lifted high and stick in hand, but he doesn't hit her, instead allowing her to bite. If your dog avoids the decoy's attack, then the latter pretends to fight with you until your dog engages him in battle. Encourage your dog with a loud "Get him, get him," and praise her when she bites.

Later on—when your dog doesn't run away from the fight—the decoy can try to chase your dog away. However, as soon as your dog bolts, the decoy has to stop to give her a chance to bite. Briefly stepping aside or going back is usually enough to increase a dog's flagging courage.

When everything works well, the decoy can try to fend off your dog's attack by hitting her with the stick. The decoy can also fire shots or throw articles toward the dog, such as pieces of plastic hose or aluminum pipes, before she reaches him and after she has bitten. These last exercises can also be trained at a distance from you, the handler.

The decoy can counter-attack by throwing pieces of rubber hose (see right above the dog).

You need to attach great value to the Out when the decoy is standing still. Never forget to praise your dog. When the exercise is over, you can take your dog away from the area or call your dog away from the decoy. When the exercises are working out well, you can connect them with the other exercises already mentioned in this chapter. Remember to vary the order in which you practice the exercises to ensure your dog doesn't get used to a set pattern.

Guarding Articles

Guarding an Article is one of the most important protection exercises, and it has great value for breeding as well as for protection work. The breeding value is that this exercise demands almost all the characteristics a good working dog must possess. No other exercise will demand so much of a dog. Here, the dog must prove her watchfulness, courage, sharpness, obedience, independence, and powers of discernment. If a dog does well in this exercise, she should be considered a fine example of her breed. The exercise Guarding an Article goes as follows.

Your dog must guard an article belonging to you, sitting or lying down beside it. To either side of her, about 6.5 feet (2 m) away, are the articles of a stranger (one on each side). The

This future protection dog guards his handler's bicycle.

decoy in bite suit tries to entice your dog away from her place. He makes two attempts to take the article she is guarding away from her. In the first attempt, he tries to quietly take the article away; in the second, he threatens her, hits her, and shoots the pistol in the air. Your dog must attack the decoy during the second attempt. The decoy will keep the dog fighting as long as they are both within 6.5 feet (2 m) of the article. Then the decoy ends the fight, and your dog has to release and immediately return to the article.

Before and after both attempts to take the article away, the decoy walks by your dog two or three times, at a distance of about 6.5 to 10 feet (2–3 m), motioning with his arms. The decoy takes the first strange article beside your dog after his first attempt to take your dog's article. He takes the other strange article after his second attempt with your dog. Your dog is not allowed to interfere in the removal of the strange articles.

Some trainers will think this exercise is impossible, but it isn't. Because of the way your dog has been trained in bite work and because of the obedience exercises she has undergone (explained in the Obedience section of this book), working out this exercise will be possible for her. Try starting the exercise the following way: Leash your dog and ask her to sit or lie down, then squat or kneel beside her and place an article replete with your odor (a cap or shirt, or something not too small) in front of her with the command "Watch him." The decoy (without bite suit) approaches your dog calmly, and slowly reaches, hesitant and fearful, for the article. Keep your dog on a short leash so she cannot reach the decoy. The best way is to fasten the line to a tree or post; this helps keep her under control. As soon as the decoy touches the article and moves it somewhat (he must not take it away), command, "Get him." If your dog lunges at the decoy, the latter quickly jumps back so the dog cannot reach him. Praise her, "Good girl, watch him, good girl," and then command, "To your place," so she will return to her spot near the article.

If your dog growls at the decoy when he moves to take the article, or if she shows her teeth before the decoy can touch the article, praise her exuberantly. The decoy should leave if this happens. After your dog has displayed teeth or growls at the decoy, the decoy knows he must now wear his protection gear when working with her. Now suited up, the decoy threatens to take the article a few times, then he makes a real grab, and your dog is allowed to bite. If she is indifferent to the decoy, then he can tease or threaten in order to incite her to bite. The decoy must skillfully avoid the dog's lunge. You also must ensure that your dog doesn't attack the decoy before he takes the article.

If it's clear that your dog has begun to understand her task, before the decoy grabs the article, he should first walk back and forth a few times in front of her, and every once in a while briefly stand still in front of her. Your dog is allowed to threaten the decoy by growling or barking, but she is not to bite him.

At the end of each exercise, the decoy walks a few times in front of your guarding dog, and he has to ensure that she is still attentive to him. If your dog is distracted for a moment, the decoy will quickly walk to the article and grab at it.

After training this way for some time, your dog can work on a long line and the decoy continues to work in bite suit. Lay your article before your dog, command, "Watch him," walk a few feet behind your dog, and firmly grip the line. The decoy first walks by the dog a few times, and then he grabs at the article, not so timid anymore. For the first little while, after the dog has bitten in, the decoy doesn't fight with the dog but stands still so that the dog releases. Then he walks away without looking at the dog. This is your cue to command your dog to once again take her place.

You don't have to insist that she bites when the decoy touches the article. If she lunges, that will be enough at first. In this exercise, the important thing is that your dog chases the decoy away after a brief bite. Don't repeat this exercise too often. If you have a very sharp dog, don't let the decoy touch the articles too often, but he should walk by her with arms swinging.

If these exercises are going as they should, the decoy can put more pressure on your dog in trying to chase her away from the article. However, he always has to be attentive to the dog's behavior. Don't be too violent with your dog, even when she seems fearless. The decoy's attempts are a bit timid at first and slowly become more aggressive. As soon as your dog has bitten in, the decoy moves the fight about 6.5 feet (2 m) away from the article and then stands still. After she releases, the decoy goes away without looking back at your dog. You must ensure that your dog goes back to her position by the article immediately after the Out, using the command "To your place." At this point, you can reward your dog.

During the next training sessions, you can advance farther away from your guarding dog. Support her less and less, until your help isn't needed anymore. But if necessary, don't hesitate to support her in her task. By this point in training, the decoy not only walks in front of your dog but also around her, or he runs with arms swinging.

The next step in training this exercise is to ask a stranger to place an article of his (e.g., a cap, handkerchief) about 10 feet (3 m) away from your guarding dog. He or she should do this; you may not touch the object. After the decoy walks by the dog several times, he picks up this strange article, without first attempting to grab the article your dog is guarding. While picking up the strange article, the decoy has to keep an eye on the dog, and you should stand close to your dog. If your dog wants to go to the decoy while he picks up the strange article, correct her with a powerful "To your place."

Now someone can lay a strange article on the other side of the dog, a bit closer now, but never closer than 6.5 feet (2 m). Later on, articles will be laid on both sides of your dog. Use these articles to teach your dog it's okay for the decoy to take objects that don't have your scent. In further training, use bigger articles such as bags, suitcases, or bicycles. After some training, your bicycle can be put between two strange bicycles, as close as possible to each other, even with the tires touching. Ask your dog to guard your bike. As always, make sure you vary the training, including the locations at which you train.

Practical Exercises

When he is helping to train a protection dog, a decoy in bite suit stimulates the dog's sharpness to a great extent. As unnatural as this bite suit seems, it's vital as a technical aid to train the dog for absolute obedience. When a dog sees a decoy in a bite suit and doesn't attack unless she receives a command from her handler, we can be sure that in real life she will do the same with unprotected people. To increase the obedience of the protection dog, practice the following real-life exercises.

A practical exercise: first through the shower, then biting the decoy.

In the exercise Apprehending a Decoy Fleeing on a Bicycle in the Dutch Police Dog test, we have often seen impressive but also dangerous bite work. These days, it is highly recommended to train the dog to bite only the decoy's leg in this test.

1. When riding in the car, a dog should lie down on the back seat, on the floor between the front and back seats, or in the open back space of a hatchback or station wagon. Have her assume her position in the car and then take up your position in the driver's seat. Now the decoy approaches the car, whose windows are down, and first has a friendly chat with you as you sit behind the steering wheel. The decoy then leaves. Later on, he returns to the car very aggressively. Depending on the situation, your dog has to behave herself quietly, attentive to the command "Out" or perhaps "Watch him," to which she may react with barking. The dog may not jump around in the car. It is not necessary to teach your dog to guard the car. A well-trained protection dog already knows to guard her handler's car, boat, or house and yard against intruders.

2. In this exercise, the decoy circles around you and your dog on a bicycle, kicking in your direction. After the command "Watch him," command, "Get him," and your dog must be trained to bite the decoy on the leg as he kicks in her direction. As soon as the dog has bitten in, the decoy lets the bicycle fall to the side opposite from your dog. Mind that the bicycle doesn't fall on the dog. If you do a Transport, you should take the bicycle with you to prevent the decoy from escaping on the bike.

3. Work out heeling or other obedience exercises with your dog while another dog does bite work training close by.

4. The decoy is fighting with one or more persons. Circle around this group, first with your dog on leash and later on, off leash. After circling, command her to wait, walk over to the fighting people, and break them up. The dog should stay in her position.

5. Command your dog to attack a decoy and, after a short fight, command "Out." Although the decoy continues to make threatening actions, your dog should not bite. When you begin training this exercise, stand close to your dog, but later on move away from her.

6. The decoy stands about 164 feet (50 m) in front of you, makes fighting movements, and fires one or more shots. Your unleashed dog has to stay with you.

7. The decoy stands about 164 feet (50 m) in front of you, makes threatening movements with a stick, and escapes. Send your dog in pursuit, and the decoy turns around, drops the stick, and stands still, facing your approaching dog. Immediately call "Out"; she may not bite. Eventually, guarding or barking at the decoy is no problem. After this, go to your dog, take her on heel, and praise her exuberantly.

8. The decoy stands about 164 feet (50 m) in front of the handler, makes threatening movements, and escapes. Send your dog to pursue and stop the decoy. When your dog has covered half or three-quarters of the distance toward the still-running decoy, command, "Out," and call her back to you. She must stop her pursuit and return to you.

By means of careful and thoughtful training, dogs can become absolutely reliable protection animals that are always under their handler's control.

You don't have to wait until your dog has mastered all the exercises in bite work to train the last two exercises. As soon as she understands what is expected of her in bite work, you can introduce them to her. The dog learns that in bite work she must strictly obey the commands of her handler, and she isn't allowed to act according to her own will or react to all stimuli from her environment. When a dog understand this, and she is absolutely controlled by her handler at all times, she can be called a safe and reliable protection dog.

Epilogue

Pets and the Working Dog

First-time dog owners often have few demands of their pet: he must be "very lovable" and, of course, "obedient"; he also has to be "alert." Furthermore, they absolutely do not want a "character dog" (by which they mean stubborn, dominant, or overactive) because those are so difficult to educate.

Unfortunately, a lot of the dog breeds that are popular with the general public have up until now been working dogs: sheepdogs, guard dogs, and protection dogs, all of which are "character" dogs that hold their ground. But that is what most people don't want anymore; they ask for lovable, devoted, pet dogs—even from those guard and protection breeds.

The public will get what they ask for. In less than 30 years, working dogs that were formerly of firm character and active temperament became, through thoughtless breeding, nervous cuddle dogs. This fits the demands of the new buyers very well, because nervous and frightened dogs firmly press themselves to their owners and are therefore "very loving." Due to their excessive submissiveness, they are most of the time slavishly servile to people and are taken to be "obedient." And because such dogs are afraid of even their own shadows, every sound will make them bark, so one concludes they are "alert" guard dogs. For sure, they bark and are

If we want our
grandchildren to know
working dogs that
still have their original
character, we need to
protect the working-
dog lines.

lovable and obedient, but for completely different reasons than
their forebears.

Breed Foundations

The required practical qualities of a dog breed were, and still
are, the foundation of most breeds. When we allow ourselves to
undermine those foundations, we do so knowing that the sturdy
buildings our predecessors constructed will eventually fall down.
Some might say, "The practical value of my breed doesn't interest me; I have my dog only as a nice pet and I don't want to train
him. Besides, in many standards, they say that the breed is an
ideal pet." In some ways, this is correct, but the sentiment is also
wrong. We have to watch that we don't throw the baby out with
the bathwater.

There are a lot of gundogs out there that never have seen game or retrieved a bird. By the same token, there are many sheepdogs that hunt sheep instead of tending them, or guard and protection dogs that have not the slightest idea how to defend against an attack. We must not exaggerate. It isn't necessary that every gun-dog, shepherd, or guard dog individually performs the work he was originally bred for. On principle, though, it is desirable that these dogs stay mentally and physically suitable for their original work, even if some of these dogs will never be working dogs.

Breed Characteristics

Even a dog with a more or less serious fault to his breed standard can be a fine dog and will without any doubt be an unforgettable friend. But the love of our own dogs should not blind us to what the breed in total has to be. All our breeds should have a certain character, a certain behavior, a certain structure, and characteristics that have a direct connection with their original work. Those spe-cific qualities demarcate the specific breeds, leave their marks on them, and should be inseparably connected to them.

A terrier has a different structure and temperament than a sheepdog because originally these two breeds were meant to do completely different things. With the dilution of the working qualities, the dog himself, in creature, character, and type, becomes diluted.

What we want to have are different dog breeds that have cer-tain characteristics. Such characteristics are directly connected with the original task for which our predecessors selected those dogs centuries ago. It is crucial that we not damage that careful selection in the space of a few years.

Or do some people really want to have a sort of "uniform" dog? In that case, we had better breed a new "family" dog for them. But let such people stay away from the working dogs. Fortunately, there are still enough people who appreciate the working dog, with all his good and distinctive characteristics.

We have much more need for less beautiful dogs that have very good and stable characters than beautiful but mentally weak and inferior dogs. We must not turn the whole ship around in order to custom fit the breeds according to the desires of pet buyers. The different dog breeds once demanded certain requirements of character and therefore certain types of owners, not the other way around.

Appendix

Dutch, German, and English Commands

International Phonetic Alphabet (IPA) Pronunciation Guide

The following guide to the IPA characters used in this appendix offers examples of English words to help you pronounce the Dutch and German ones. The portion of the English word that provides the pronunciation clue is given in italics.

: = indicates preceding sound is long; for example, u: = bl*ue*
ʻ = indicates what syllable is stressed in the word

ɑ = *a*far
ɐ = c*au*ght
ɔ = *ou*ght
ç = *h*ue, lo*ch*
j = *y*ard
ŋ = lo*ng*
ʊ = b*oo*ks
ø: = roughly like h*u*rt
ʃ = *sh*all
ʌ = c*u*t
ɐ̯ = comm*a*
ɛ = l*e*t
ɪ = s*i*t
n̩ = butt*on*
aʊ = h*ow*
œ = roughly like h*u*g
œy = roughly like h*ou*se
ə = red*u*ction
y = roughly like c*u*te

Dutch Commands

Command	Pronunciation	English
Achter	ɑxtər	Rear, Behind, Back
Af	ɑf	Down
Apport	ɑpɔrt	Bring, Fetch, Retrieve
Blijf	blɛif	Stay
Braaf	braf	Good dog
Breed	bret	Jump (wide)
Foei	fuj	No, stop it
Goed zo	gutzo	Good boy, Good girl
Halt	hɑlt	Stop
Hier	hir	Come
Hoog	hox	Hup, Jump (high)
Kom	kɔm	Come
Kom er uit	kɔm ər œyt	Come out
Kom voor	kɔm vor	Come-fore
Kruip	krœyp	Crawl
Let op	lɛt ɔp	Watch, Watch him/her, Guard
Links	lɪŋ(k)s	Heel (to the) left
Los	lɔs	Out
Luid	lœyt	Bark, Loud, Search
Nee	ne	No, Don't
Plaats	plats	To your place, Down
Rechts	rɛxs	Heel (to the) right
Revier	rə'vir	Search
Spring	sprɪŋ	Hup, Jump (high)
Sta	sta	Stand, Stop
Stellen	stɛlə	Get him
Stil	stɪl	Quiet, Silent
Terug	tə'rʌg	Back
Vast	vɑst	Get him
Voet	vut	Heel
Volg	vɔləg	Heel

Get him; Fass, Stellen, Vast.

Vooruit	'vo'rœyt	Go, Go out, Go on
Vrij	vrɛi	Free
Wachten	wɑxtə	Wait, Stay
Zit	zɪt	Sit
Zoek	zuk	Seek, Search
Zwijg	zwɛig	Quiet, Silent

German Commands

Command	Pronunciation	English
Apport	ɑpɔrt	Bring, Fetch, Retrieve
Aus	aus	Out
Bei Fuss	bai fu:s	Come to heel, Heel
Bleib	'blaib	Stay
Brav	bra:f	Good dog
Breit	brait	Jump (wide)
Fass	fas	Get him
Folgen'	'fɔlgn̩	Heel
Frei	frai	Free
Fuss	fu:s	Heel
Gib Acht	'gi:p axt	Watch, Watch him/her, Guard

Gib Laut	ˈgiːp laut	Bark, Loud, Search
Guter Hund	guːtɐ hʊnt	Good dog
Halt	halt	Stop
Heraus	hɛˈraus	Come out
Herein	hɛˈrain	Come-fore
Hier	hiːɐ̯	Come
Hopp	hɔp	Hup, Jump (high)
Kriech ˈ	ˈkriːç	Crawl
Laut	laut	Bark, Loud, Search
Links folgen	lɪŋks ˈfɔlgn̩	Heel (to the) left
Nein	ˈnain	No, Don't
Pass auf	pas auf	Watch, Watch him/her
Pfui	auf	No, Stop it
Platz	plats	Down
Rechts folgen	rɛçts ˈfɔlgn̩	Heel (to the) right
Revier	reˈviːɐ̯	Search, Find
Sitz	zɪts	Sit
So brav	zoː braːf	Good dog
Spur	ʃpuːɐ̯	Rear, Behind, Back
Steh	ˈʃteː	Stand, Stop
Stellen	ˈʃtɛlən	Get him
Still	ʃtɪl	Quiet, Silent

Good dog; Brav, Guter Hund, Braaf, Goed zo.

Stöbern	ˈʃtø:bɐn	Seek, Search (with high nose)
Such	ˈzu:x	Seek, Search
Voran	foˈran	Go, Go out, Go on
Warten	ˈvartn̩	Wait, Stay
Zurück	tsuˈrʏk	Back

English Commands

Command	German	Dutch
Back	Zurück	Terug
(Walk) Back	Spur	Achter
Bark	(Gib) Laut	Luid
Behind	Spur	Achter
Bring	Apport	Apport
Come	Herein, Hier	Hier, Kom
Come-fore	Komm vor, Hier	Kom voor
Come out	Heraus	Kom er uit
Come to heel	Bei Fuss, Fuss	Voet, Volg
Crawl	Kriech	Kruip
Don't	Nein	Nee
Down	Platz	Af
Fetch	Apport	Apport
Find	Revier	Revier
Free	Frei	Vrij
Get him	Fass, Stellen	Vast, Stellen
Good dog	(So) Brav, Guter Hund	Braaf, Goed zo
Go, Go out, Go on	Voran	Vooruit
Guard	Gib Acht	Let op
Heel	(Bei) Fuss, Folgen	Voet, Volg
Heel (to the) left	Links folgen	Links volgen
Heel (to the) right	Rechts folgen	Rechts volgen
Hup	Hopp	Hoog, Spring
Jump (high)	Hopp	Hoog, Spring
Jump (wide)	Breit	Breed
Loud	(Gib) Laut	Luid

No, Don't	Nein	Nee
No, Stop it	Pfui	Foei
Out	Aus	Los
(To your) Place	Platz	Plaats
Quiet	Still	Stil, Zwijg
Rear	Spur	Achter
Retrieve	Apport	Apport
Search (bark)	(Gib) Laut	Luid
Search (person)	Revier	Revier
Search (high nose)	Stöbern	Zoeken
Search (track)	Such	Zoek
Seek	Such	Zoek
Silent	Still	Stil, Zwijg
Sit	Sitz	Zit
Stand	Steh	Sta
Stay	Bleib, Warten	Blijf, Wachten
Stop	Halt	Halt
Stop it	Pfui	Foei
To your place	Platz	Plaats
Wait	Warten	Wachten
Watch (him/her)	Gib Acht, Pass Auf	Let op

Bibliography

American Kennel Club. 1992. *The Complete Dog Book*. New York: Howell Book House.

Army Headquarters. 1977. *Military Police Working Dogs*. Washington, DC.

Barwig, S., and S. Hilliard. 1991. *Schutzhund: Theory and Training Methods*. New York: Howell Book House.

Böttger, P. 1937. *Hunde im Dienste der Kriminalpolizei*. Berlin: Zeitschrift für Hundeforschung.

Bryson, S. 2000. *Police Dog Tactics*. Calgary, AB: Detselig Enterprises, Ltd.

Dalziel, H. 1909. *Breaking and Training Dogs*. London, UK: L. Upcott Gill.

Eden, R.S. 1997. *K9 Officer's Manual*. Calgary, AB: Detselig Enterprises, Ltd.

Eden, R.S. 1999. *Dog Training for Law Enforcement*. Calgary, AB: Detselig Enterprises, Ltd.

Grandjean, D. 2000. *Practical Guide for Sporting and Working Dogs*. Aimargues, France: Royal Canin.

Haak, R. 1984. *Het Africhten tot Verdedigingshond*. Best, the Netherlands: Zuid Boekprodukties.

Haak, R. 1988. *Honden en Hun Gedrag*. Best, the Netherlands: Zuid Boekprodukties.

Haberhauffe, L., and G. Albrecht. 1982. *Schutz- und Diensthunde*. Melsungen, Germany: Verlag J. Neumann-Neudamm.

Hartman, D. 1991. *Honden Leren Sorteren en Speuren*. Best, the Netherlands: Zuid Boekprodukties.

Henze, O. 1926. *Die Erziehung und Abrichtung des Hundes*. Berlin: Kameradschaftsverlag.

Kaldenbach, J. 1998. *K9 Scent Detection: My Favorite Judge Lives in a Kennel*. Calgary, AB: Detselig Enterprises, Ltd.

Lorenz, K. 1978. *Vergleichende Verhaltensforschung: Grundlagen der Ethologie*. Wien: Springer. http://dx.doi.org/10.1007/978-3-7091-3097-1.

Mackenzie, S.A. 1996. *Decoys and Aggression: A Police K9 Training Manual.* Calgary, AB: Detselig Enterprises, Ltd.

Menzel, R., and R. Menzel. 1930. *Die Verwertung der Riechfähigkeit des Hundes im Dienste der Menschheit.* Berlin: Kameradschaftsverlag.

Mistafa, R. 1998. *K9 Explosive Detection: A Manual for Trainers.* Calgary, AB: Detselig Enterprises, Ltd.

Most, K. 1977. *Training Dogs: A Manual.* London, UK: Popular Dogs.

Raiser, H. 1981. *Der Schutzhund.* Hamburg: Paul Parey Verlag.

Richardson, E.H. 1923. *Watch-Dogs: Their Training and Management.* London, UK: Hutchinson & Co.

Schmidt, F. 1910. *Verbrecherspur und Polizeihund.* Augsburg, Germany: Selbstverlag SV.

Schmidt, F. 1911. *Polizeihund-Erfolge und Neue Winke.* Augsburg, Germany: Selbstverlag SV.

Stark, C. 1998. *A Dog Is Not a Gun: Observations on Canine Policing.* Calgary, AB: Detselig Enterprises, Ltd.

Zimen, E. 1971. *Wölfe und Konigspudel, Vergleichende Verhaltensbeobuchtungen.* München, Germany: Piper und Co.

About the Authors

Ruud Haak is the author of more than 30 dog books in Dutch and German. Since 1979 he has been the editor-in-chief of the biggest Dutch dog magazine, *Onze Hond (Our Dog)*. He was born in 1947 in Amsterdam, the Netherlands. At the age of 13, he was training police dogs at his uncle's security dog training center, and when he was 15 he worked after school with his patrol dog (which he trained himself) at the Amsterdam harbor. He later started training his dogs in Schutzhund and IPO and successfully bred and trained German shepherd dogs.

Ruud worked as a social therapist in a government clinic for criminal psychopaths. From his studies in psychology, he became interested in dog behavior and training methods for nose work, especially the tracking dog (Fährtenhund) and the search and rescue (SAR) dog. More recently he has trained drug and explosive detector dogs for the Dutch police and the Royal Dutch Airforce. He is also a visiting lecturer at Dutch, German, and Austrian police dog schools.

In the 1970s, Ruud and his wife, Dr. Resi Gerritsen, a psychologist and jurist, attended many courses and symposia with their German shepherds for Schutzhund, tracking dog, and SAR dog training in Switzerland, Germany, and Austria. In 1979 they started the Dutch Rescue Dog Organization in the Netherlands.

Ruud Haak and his dogs.

Dr. Resi Gerritsen and her dogs.

With that unit, they attended many operations responding to earthquakes, gas explosions, and lost persons in wilderness areas. In 1990 Ruud and Resi moved to Austria, where they were asked by the Austrian Red Cross to select and train operational SAR and avalanche dogs. They lived for three years at a height of 6000 feet (1800 m) in the Alps and worked with their dogs in search missions in the wake of avalanches.

With their Austrian colleagues, Ruud and Resi developed a new method for training SAR dogs. This way of training showed the best results after a major earthquake in Armenia (1988), and earthquakes in Japan (1995), Turkey (1999), and Algeria and Iran (2003), as well as many subsequent big earthquakes and other major events. Ruud and Resi have also demonstrated the success of their unique training methods at National and World Championships, where both were several times the leading champions.

Resi and Ruud have held many symposia and master classes all over the world on their unique training methods, which are featured in their books:

> *K9 Search and Rescue: Training the Natural Way*
>
> *K9 Professional Tracking: A Complete Manual for Theory and Training*
>
> *K9 Complete Care: A Manual for Physically and Mentally Healthy Working Dogs*
>
> *K9 Working Breeds: Characteristics and Capabilities*
>
> *K9 Fraud: Fraudulant Handling of Police Dogs*
>
> *K9 Scent Training: A Manual for Training Your Identification, Tracking and Detection Dog*
>
> *K9 Schutzhund Training: A Manual for IPO Training through Positive Reinforcement*

With Simon Prins they wrote *K9 Behavior Basics: A Manual for Proven Success in Operational Service Dog Training*; and with Dr. Adee Schoon, Ruud wrote *K9 Suspect Discrimination: Training and Practicing Scent Identification Line-ups*. All of these books were published by Detselig Enterprises, Ltd., in Calgary, Canada (now Brush Education Inc.).

Ruud and Resi now live in the Netherlands. They are training directors and international judges for the International Red Cross

Federation, the United Nations (OCHA), the International Rescue Dog Organisation (IRO), and the Fédération Cynologique Internationale (FCI).

At the moment Ruud and Resi are still successfully training their dogs as detector dogs for SAR, drugs, explosives, and in IPO and protection dog training. You can contact the authors by e-mail at: onzehond@bcm.nl

K9 Professional Training series

K9 Professional Training Series

K9 Scent Training
A Manual for Training Your Identification, Tracking and Detection Dog
Resi Gerritsen • Ruud Haak
K9 PROFESSIONAL TRAINING SERIES

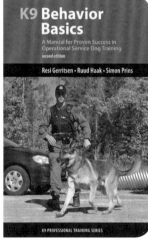

K9 Behavior Basics
A Manual for Proven Success in Operational Service Dog Training
second edition
Resi Gerritsen • Ruud Haak • Simon Prins
K9 PROFESSIONAL TRAINING SERIES

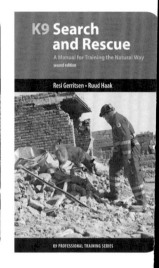

K9 Search and Rescue
A Manual for Training the Natural Way
second edition
Resi Gerritsen • Ruud Haak
K9 PROFESSIONAL TRAINING SERIES

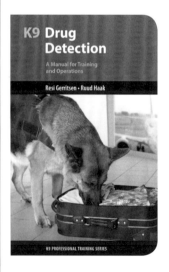

K9 Drug Detection
A Manual for Training and Operations
Resi Gerritsen • Ruud Haak
K9 PROFESSIONAL TRAINING SERIES

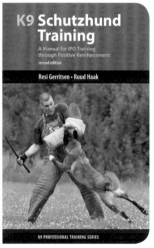

K9 Schutzhund Training
A Manual for IPO Training through Positive Reinforcement
second edition
Resi Gerritsen • Ruud Haak
K9 PROFESSIONAL TRAINING SERIES

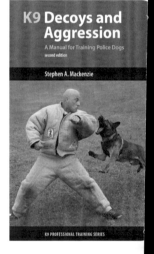

K9 Decoys and Aggression
A Manual for Training Police Dogs
second edition
Stephen A. Mackenzie
K9 PROFESSIONAL TRAINING SERIES